THE
GRADGATE

Why You Are More Employable Than You Think

YOUSEF SHADID

Headshot photography: Mohammad Othman (Othman Media)

Interior formatting and cover design: Shabbir Hussain (Access Ideas)

ISBN: 978-0-6450809-2-6

I dedicate this book to every graduate who
feels clueless, frustrated or simply lost with their job search.
May this open as many GradGates as possible for you.

CONTENTS

INTRODUCTION

I. Why Are You Here?

One morning during my second year of business studies, I attended a lecture on statistics and data analytics. There were about 60 of us inside the lecture theatre, but it was clear that some of us were not paying attention.

The lecturer asked us, *'Why are you studying here? What is the purpose of you being at university?'* As basic as this question sounded, none of us voiced a clear answer!

She continued, *'Why are you paying for your education?'*

'Cause it's good for us', someone yelled from the back row.

'Of course it is, but there is more to it!' she responded. *'You are here to get a job once you graduate. Someone decided that you should be here, be it your families or yourselves, and that person wanted you here because they believe with a good education, you will get a job! Do you even want to get a job? Your lack of attention certainly tells me otherwise! You are here to get a job, so pay attention to your classes!'*

Although I found her remarks interesting, they weren't really unheard of. I mean, we all want to get jobs, right? But the reality is, I would still spend the next few semesters at university not doing a whole lot to achieve that goal.

Why?

My understanding (and for that matter, most students' understanding) was that I should only start worrying about getting a job towards graduation. Little did I know that this type of thinking was the exact reason why many graduates struggle with finding jobs.

II. It's All About Perspective

Do all graduates land jobs? No. Does everyone in the job market have a degree? Also no. But students start their degree with the underlying assumption that it will lead to a job. A few are vocal and proactive about it, while the majority of students just keep it as an assumption until they approach the finish line— graduation.

Regardless of where you are in your graduate journey, I'd like to ask you to always keep your perspective in check. I know that many of us have struggled (or are struggling) to find a job. But this shouldn't be the case. Yes, there's a solution to the struggle— your perspective.

Your ability to change your perspective and keep it in check is your superpower! Positions are created and abolished. Jobs come and go. Employees get promoted and demoted. Salaries increase and decrease. Companies rise and collapse. Degrees are taught and forgotten. Economies prosper and plummet. Money is earned and spent. Do you notice a pattern here? The only constant in all of these is *change*.

While some of these changes are beyond your control, you do have one thing that is under your control 100% of the time: YOUR PERSPECTIVE.

'*Is finding a job difficult?*'

'*Is it easy?*'

'*Is having average grades enough to land me a job?*'

'Can I get a graduate position at an international firm?'

'What about the Big-4 Management Consulting firms?'

'Would any company hire me without experience?'

'I think I chose the wrong course.'

'It's getting so competitive in the job market, and finding a graduate job post-COVID? Forget about it!'

Chances are you have heard or made most, if not all of these statements in the past. Still, I believe it's a matter of perspective. While I don't deny that some of these statements will be true at the time, we tend to make them based on our feelings and NOT facts.

The same goes for the statement: 'It's so difficult to get a job.' While it's true that some graduates tend to have a more difficult time in finding a job than others, such a statement is usually based on a person's perspective.

Yes, I know. You're probably thinking, 'I just want to get a job. I don't need theory!' or 'That's easy for you to say because you already have a job.' But just bear with me here. I want to explain why getting a graduate job is actually easier than you may think.

Before we get deep into it, I want to know where you're coming from first. What do you hope to get out of reading this book?

You're probably here because you want to get some tips on finding and landing a job. If I'm right, keep on reading. But if you're someone who's fixed on the idea that finding a graduate job is nearly impossible, you have to change your perspective before reading on. I know that you may have had experiences in the past that suggest otherwise. But in order for you to get the most out of this book, you need to open your mind. BELIEVE that it's possible, that it can be easy to land a graduate job.

If you don't, you may still get some value out of this. However, you may not end up taking the actions required to excel and get your dream role.

Regardless of what your opinion is right now, and what lessons you will learn and unlearn from this book, remember that your perspective is your superpower. The benefits of having the right mindset go beyond landing a job. It can also impact the different areas of life, from finances to relationships, and other major life events.

III. Are You Lost?

If you ask me, I sure was. To say that I was '*very lost*' is putting it lightly.

I switched courses and majors twice, and it took me almost six years to graduate. I also changed casual jobs five times during my studies. Other than that, I deferred my studies for some time so that I could travel. (No regrets with this decision, by the way.) So, how's that for being lost?

Actually, I'd like to share with you a quick summary of my graduate journey. That way, you know exactly where I'm coming from when I say that I was once in your shoes too. Hopefully, by the end of this section, you know that I'm just like you and that my goal is to help you land that dream job.

As someone who did a fair bit of Mathematics and Physics in high school, taking up engineering '*made sense*' for me. So, I enrolled in a double degree of Bachelor of Engineering (Civil) / Bachelor of Business, at Swinburne University of Technology. Double degrees weren't as common back then, but it made perfect sense how they would make me more '*employable*'.

My degree was my choice. I didn't have any pressure from family or friends. But I was told that a technical degree is always a 'safe option' when it comes to getting a job later on. To be honest, I was fairly content with my choice back then, even if I wasn't passionate about it or didn't fully understand its career prospects.

I remember during Orientation Week (O-Week), the Course Coordinator ran us through the course structure and the different majors that we could take. While some students knew exactly what to take and how to go about it, most of us started asking all sorts of questions about career outcomes.

It was a lengthy Q&A session. The Course Coordinator discussed career prospects such as becoming a Site Engineer, Structural Engineer, Project Manager and so on. He concluded with this statement, *'To all the students in the hall, I ask you to look to the persons to your right and left. Get to know them. According to the faculty statistics, in a couple of years, only one of you three will graduate from this degree. The rest will either transfer degrees or drop-out of uni altogether.'*

Now, as a first-year student, that statement got me thinking, *'Why do people change degrees? Isn't everyone here comfortable with their choice? Why would someone start a degree if they are not planning to finish it?'*

Still, the course coordinator's statement gave me great comfort. It assured me that I wasn't the only one uncertain about the degree and where it would lead.

Moving on, I pursued my studies for the next two years. After all, why would I change if things were going well and I was 'guaranteed a job'? But to the disappointment of my parents and I, I DID end up changing my degree soon after. I dropped engineering and focused on business. Was I confident that it's *'what I was passionate about'*? Not exactly. But I was sure that I didn't like or enjoy engineering. My grades had also started to reflect my feelings. So, I had to do something. I had to change my degree.

I was happy to take that leap of faith even if I believed that my previous degree had better job prospects (a belief I can spend hours debating now).

In search of a business major, I chose accounting and with management as my minor. Three years and two exchange semesters later, I graduated with a credit average.

While graduating was an achievement by itself, rejection was also a recurring theme in my final year. Aiming to secure a job within my field, I polished my resume, attended some job fairs and even paid a visit to the Careers Office. I sent out over a hundred job applications to increase my chances. But guess what happened? I got rejected from all of them. Despite the time and effort I put in, I never got positive feedback. Some didn't even give me any response at all. It was VERY frustrating. The fact that other students had already secured their roles didn't help. Don't get me wrong. I was happy for them, but I became really frustrated. I felt lost.

So, if you're lost, frustrated or both, it's okay. I was too. The great thing is if I could find a job after all that, so can you! And I can help you do that through this book. Here, I share what I've learnt over the years that made me more *'employable'*. If you apply these on your journey, you'll be able to deal competently with rejection or, better yet, avoid it altogether and land your dream job!

IV. The GradGate

Have you been wondering what GradGate means? It's a combination of the definitions of **Grad** and **Gate**.

Grad: *Short for Graduate (informal): a person who has a university degree.*

Gate: *[countable] a barrier like a door that is used to close an opening in a fence or a wall outside a building.*

Put together, GradGate pertains to the doors of employability. These are the doors that open to possibilities including your dream role.

Open Your GradGate!

Yes! We will open your GradGate! To do that, I need you to see the role it plays in your journey first. And by '*see*', I want you to imagine with me right now.

Imagine yourself standing on this huge mass of land. It's your home. (Let's call it a continent.) Suddenly, you find yourself standing by a shore. You look around and find hundreds, if not thousands, of strangers. As you try to find your bearings, someone tells you about an island outside the continent. It's filled with resources. (Let's call it '*The Island*'.) It's said that only a few people can get there at any time, and the ships that travel there have limited seating. But you pay no attention to The Island. It doesn't interest you because the continent provides everything you need.

Afterwards, some of the strangers you saw earlier rush to a nearby harbour. They want to get to The Island. To do that, they enter through a boarding gate at the port so they can hop on a docked ship. Nearby, you notice another group of people going in the same direction. Unlike the first group, they're not in a rush. They're just walking. Despite these, The Island still doesn't appeal to you. You continue living on the continent, enjoying all that it has to offer. You even make friends with some of the strangers you saw at the beginning.

As the months pass by, you hear stories of people discovering other harbours scattered around the continent. Some of these don't have boarding gates. You also learn that some of your colleagues have left the continent. They went to find their version of The Island, with several reporting that the islands they found are just as good as The Island, if not better.

Intrigued, you decide to tag along on one of these trips. You go through one of those harbours with boarding gates at its ports. Enthusiasm fills you as you start the journey. But midway through your trip, your boat starts sinking. You have to jump ship and swim to survive. After hours of struggling with the waves, you manage to swim back to the continent. You're dehydrated and extremely fatigued. In deep frustration, you swear that you will never do it again.

(You've stretched your imagination this far. Bear with me on this last bit! We're almost there!)

As the years go by, you become fairly comfortable living on the continent. You establish your social groups, habits and even territories. In fact, you're so comfortable now that you barely explore other parts of the continent, let alone check other harbours or any islands offshore.

Then one day, as if in an action-adventure series, you wake up to the news that a nearby volcano will soon erupt. No one knows how much time there is to act, but your best guess is a few weeks at most. Panicked, you head towards the nearest port. However, you see a long queue at the gate, so you decide to leave before it's too late. You jump in the water and start swimming away from the continent with no destination in mind. Finally, after hours of swimming, you arrive on a tiny island.

Did you see the symbolisms in the story? As you probably guessed, you and the rest of the strangers are *the graduates*. The continent is your *university*. The Island that everyone sought to see? It's your *dream job*.

What about all the resources you had on the continent? Those would be your connections, activities, involvement, networks, and the knowledge you build on-campus. Your failed attempt to see one of the islands? That's you trying to get *work experience* to add to your application. Your so-called social group? Those are your mates, besties, fellow graduates and colleagues on-campus. The volcano? That's your *graduation date* approaching, with you only paying attention in your final year or semester. The queuing and the swimming to the tiny island? That is your *job application*, compiled in a survival mood, just to get you any job. And the tiny island? It's *any job*.

Did we miss something? Yes, those gates you kept finding at each port. Do you know what they represent? Yep, you guessed it right! Those are the *GradGates* that you want to open, or avoid if you know where they are.

The people in the story you just read left at different times. Also, not everyone went through the GradGates. But eventually, everyone left the continent with the majority waiting up to the last moment.

In the real world, this translates to students leaving university to enter the job market. Those that secure graduate jobs before everyone else might not necessarily have the best grades or know the right people. But they simply recognise the journey early enough and do what is required. Unfortunately, for the rest, they wait until their final year or even the months leading to the graduation date to search for a job. At this stage, they end up looking for *'any job'*.

V. It's The Journey AND The Destination

'Success is a journey, not a destination.' - Unknown

You have probably heard this quote before, and while it holds some truth, I prefer to say, *'Success is a journey AND a destination.'*

As a student, you are successful if you put in the effort, and even more so if you get good grades. You may consider yourself successful as a job seeker if you are proactive and dedicated, but getting hired guarantees that. As a graduate, your family and mentors consider you as successful if you complete your chosen degree. But you may only agree with them once you land your dream job (or create one as an entrepreneur, but that's a story for another time).

While we may be led to believe that our graduate journey starts upon graduation, or at best, in our final year of studies, this could not be further from the truth. It starts from the very first day of your higher education, if not before that.

Have you ever wondered how some of your university colleagues managed to do multiple internships BEFORE their final year of study? How about a graduate you know who had to turn down a couple of job offers before accepting a position on their own terms? And how all of this is happening while you struggle to get an interview?

If the questions resonated with you, let me give you the answer. First, look at the graph below. Check which grad are you and where you are in the graduate journey.

Which Grad Are You?

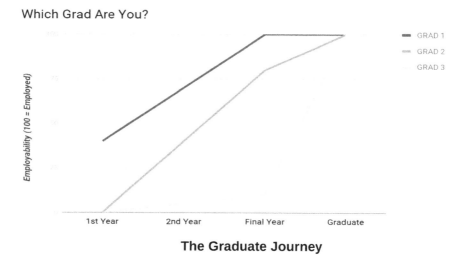

The Graduate Journey

GRAD 1 - This grad always knew what they wanted to do. They got in their course of choice and secured a job months, if not years, before graduation! They may or may not have 'known the right people'. But what they knew for sure is that finding a job was not an issue (e.g. medical students who would be in placements long before graduation).

GRAD 2 - This grad didn't always know what kind of job they wanted. But they were so curious and persistent to grow and asked the right questions that they eventually secured employment before graduation. They even had many options to choose from. This grad did not exactly 'know the right people' at the start of their studies. But they seized every opportunity to increase their knowledge and network.

GRAD 3 - This grad took up their degree because 'it seemed all right' or they just took a chance. Unfortunately, they didn't feel like what they learnt related to the job market. This grad also didn't know what their job prospects were, let alone a job they could secure. Yes, they knew the industry, but they didn't have any clue where to start looking. They only started the very act of finding a job either during their final year, just before graduation or even afterwards.

* ⚜ *

If you're **GRAD 1**, you're probably not reading this book. If you are, good on you! I'm sure you'll still get some value here. Just keep reading. If you want, you can also skip to Chapter 4, which discusses the different types of graduate journeys including graduate insights from five professionals.

If you're **GRAD 2**, you'll get some value from this book, especially if you're actively searching for jobs. Chapter 3 will be particularly helpful and useful for you.

If you're **GRAD 3**, welcome to the club! This book is for you! After reading this, I'm confident that you will turn into GRAD 2 or even GRAD 1. It all depends where you are in your graduate journey.

To open as many GradGates as possible for you, (i.e. YOU get to select which job offer you like from a pool of offers based on the skills you have), this book takes you on a journey from the very start of your degree until you graduate and find a job. As such, it is divided into four chapters.

GRAD**GATE** - **G**row, **A**cquire, **T**arget and **E**mbrace.

1. **Grow** your network and skills. More importantly, focus on your personal growth (1st YEAR).

2. **Acquire** employable skills by asking a lot of questions about your degree, courses, skills, career and job prospects (2nd YEAR).

3. **Target** your time and energy towards a specific set of skills, roles and jobs (FINAL YEAR).

4. **Embrace** the uniqueness of your journey. Always keep your perspective in check (GRADUATE).

To make things simple, let's roll with the assumption that you just started university. You're a first-year student with no idea of what to do or what employability even means. Now that we've established that, let's grow together!

GROW | ACQUIRE | TARGET | EMBRACE

CHAPTER 1

GROW
(1st YEAR)

If you were anything like me when I first got to university, you'd be clueless. You won't know what's going on because everything is new. But even if that's the case, it's fun to explore the new world you're in and meet new people. Your family and friends expect you to *have it figured out*. But the truth is, your knowledge of study options - let alone the graduate job market - is limited.

You see, everything was clear before starting university. Your primary and secondary schools designed mandatory attendance and assessment completion policies. You just needed to comply so you can proceed to the next grade. The system was clear. You didn't have to figure your way through it. The only downside to this is you didn't have much freedom. You had to do tasks as scheduled. But now, it's different.

Now that you're done with Year 12, you're in an exploration mode. Everything is new and exciting. For the first time in your life, you don't HAVE to do something or be somewhere! While there are certain mandatory university classes along with some levels of assessment you need to pass, entering university still gives you a much higher level of flexibility than ever before. This means you may even skip some lectures and still pass or even do well in a specific unit!

But just to be clear, I'm NOT suggesting that you do such. Your academic performance matters. I'm simply stating the fact that you, as a first-year student, have full autonomy now. You control your time, energy and, most importantly, your career! Even if there are outside influences coming from your partner, family, friends and peers, you have the final say. YOU decide what you want to do from here on.

So, whether you may have little or no idea about what the outcome of your degree will be (GRAD 3), or you feel 100% confident about your path (GRAD 1), or perhaps you're in between (GRAD 2), your graduate journey started the moment you attended your orientation.

Make the most of your exploration mode. Aim to grow as much as you can in terms of your skills and network. Except for the predetermined subjects during your first semester, everything from the units you take to the people you meet is within your control. Take advantage of that freedom. Do everything and anything! (Well, not anything, but you know what I mean).

Your mission to **GROW** has begun!

1.1 Network, Network, Network!

You will hear me speak quite a bit about networking. As a matter of fact, I mention this critical skill in all four chapters. I strongly believe it is the single most important skill any professional should have, let alone a graduate establishing themselves.

What is networking? It does have different meanings depending on the context. For the purpose of this journey, let's go with one of Cambridge Dictionary's definitions:

Network (verb): *To meet people who might be useful to know, especially in your job.*

I think the idea is clear here. Networking is your best friend whether you're looking to build relationships, know more about uni life, or get a job.

Your network is your *'net'-'work'*. It's the web of connections you've made up until starting university. It consists of the people you know either personally or through your family and friends.

Surely, you have heard the phrase: *'It's not what you know. It's who you know.'* Well, it's true! While your knowledge is definitely essential in the job market, your connections can make things happen for you. Again, I'm not saying that what you know is irrelevant. But based on my experience, I can assure you that who you know is more relevant to you as a person and your future career.

Networking comes in different forms. I will talk about this in detail in the coming chapters. For now, I want you to start thinking about it.

As mentioned above, the people you know make up your network. These include your relatives, friends and other social groups you joined in school or the community. Everyone you know so far is part of your existing network, whether you see them often or not.

Make sure you stay connected with as many of them as possible. This is especially true when it comes to your high school friends. But you don't have to communicate with all of them daily unless you want to. Just make sure you keep that connection, whether that means a yearly reunion or a Facebook comment every few months. Don't let a year go by without making any contact. Use the tools within your reach such as social media. I will discuss more about this powerful tool later on. But for now, just remember to use it. It can do wonders to your network.

So, you just gained access to an extensive network both socially and professionally. Act accordingly. Engage in conversations and establish quality friendships from quality interactions.

While I can't possibly cover every social setting, one great tip I can give you to build your network is to read, '*How to Win Friends and Influence People*' by Dale Carnegie. Absorb the teachings and action his advice.

On that, having someone in your network does not necessarily mean being best friends with them. The quality of each relationship you have will undoubtedly differ between people. But often, quantity matters as much as the quality of your connections. The number of people within your network matters just as much the quality of relationship you have with each of them (More about this in the next chapter).

I will conclude this section by mentioning that most, if not all, graduates who find 'good jobs' and advance in their respective fields of choice have one thing in common: **A network**. They are genuinely good at connecting with people and grow their networks early in their graduate journey.

So, I hope you are convinced that the ability to connect with people and expand your network is a vital component of your professional brand. It's vital to your career. And as I said before, your graduate journey starts during your first year. So, get to work and start building those connections!

1.2 O-Week

The Orientation Week (O-Week) is said to be the best experience for many students. It usually takes place a week or two before classes start. During O-Week, you have camps, parties, on-campus clubs & societies events like the Clubs and Societies Fair. It's a great time to meet a lot of new people and have new experiences.

If you're reading this before O-Week, make sure you attend it. Put the extra effort to be there. Participate in the activities. It's your golden chance to know everything about your university! Learn what the different faculties, classes and degrees offered are. Meet colleagues and make new connections. Immerse yourself in everything O-Week has to offer.

For my part, I admit that I was a shy first-year student. I attended sessions 'only when I had to' during Orientation Week. Still, I did find a lot of information useful. I learnt about my engineering course, on-campus accommodation options and some volunteering opportunities.

Whether you're shy like I was or more eager to mingle, attend O-Week. I can't stress it enough. If you're looking to build those employable skills early on, you need to start during orientation. Before we go further, let me define what *'employable skills'* means. It refers to the skills that increase a graduate's possibility of getting hired, in other words, getting a job.

Now, back to where we were. Remember your number one priority: Getting out there. Participate in activities and meet people. The more you know your university and its people, the more you can achieve during and after your studies.

Let me tell you about another O-Week I attended. It was during a study abroad program in my second year. (More about exchange in Chapter 2) The host institution decided that O-Week was mandatory. Although I saw the value in attending the orientation, it wasn't enough of a reason for me to change my pre-booked plane tickets. I wrote to them asking for an exemption, only to be met with clear resistance. I was stunned by their response. It detailed many disadvantages for non-attendance such as lack of accommodation options and missed campus tours. As a result, I changed my mind and paid the difference for the flights just to be there. And I'm glad I did.

When I finally arrived and attended the Orientation Week, I got to:

- meet local & international students (who later became my best friends)
- know about my subject options (with some I changed to balance the load)
- see the sporting facilities on-campus (which saved me from the expensive options off-campus)
- sign up with social clubs and for on-campus activities (which rid me of FOMO before it even became a thing)
- meet 'travelling buddies' (which completely transformed my exchange experience).

The formula worked! I was able to do more, see more and experience more. I grew my network and enjoyed my experience a lot more than I would have, had I skipped the orientation.

In the following weeks that semester, I met students from different courses and backgrounds. When I asked how they got to know each other, the answer was almost always 'O-Week'.

It's true that the exchange student life is different in many ways. But the message is still the same: DO NOT MISS O-WEEK!

1.3 Honeymoon Phase

A few weeks into the semester, you can probably say that you know the campus inside out. You know the faculty you belong to, the course you're majoring in and the sequence of your subjects for the year.

I bet you've also been hearing stories of some students taking 10 subjects in a year and others planning to go abroad. Aside from that, there are constant talks of student clubs and campus parties. You're also meeting students from different backgrounds. Everything about campus life piques your interest. It's like being in a Honeymoon Phase with university life because it's pretty much all that you think, hear and talk about. Am I right?

But I'm going to make another bet. There are a few topics you hear nothing of, mainly because these are not technically about campus life. Nevertheless, these are very important in your graduate journey. I'm talking about graduate jobs, job readiness and employability.

You might ask, *'Why would I think about those when I've just started my studies?'* I understand. Finding work may not exactly be on the list of your priorities right now.

Even if you've had some exposure to the workforce through the casual / part-time jobs you did, anything about the job market is a distant thought for you. As such, your knowledge about it is limited at this stage. And you're fine with that. After all, you're just a first-year student. You're at the Honeymoon Phase. You want to enjoy it. You can just think about your graduate journey and job security later on since it's still really early. Right? Wrong!

Yes, your first few months on campus is a time to have fun. So, go ahead. Enjoy! However, don't forget to make some conscious decisions that will help you further down the track in your graduate journey. Remember that your journey started during O-Week.

1.4 Know Thy Uni!

If you know all the social hotspots and places to be on campus by now, good for you. You can get to be where the action is. But don't forget your graduate journey. Familiarise yourself with everything your university has to offer, even if it includes places or topics you don't exactly consider fun (e.g. Careers Centre, degree specifics and colleagues). **Know Thy Uni!**

1.4.1. Careers Centre

As someone who spent a fair bit of his time participating in activities on campus, I felt like I knew it all! Well, I was wrong. I didn't know that we had a Careers Centre on campus. I didn't even know universities provided such a service. It took me until my final year to discover it! It's possible that there was a Careers Centre presentation during O-Week, but I completely missed it. Regardless, it's not something that comes up in conversations unless you're in your final year.

So, what's a Career Centre? It's basically a university department or service that's designed to help you find a job. It's also known as Jobs Centre, Professional Centre, Training and Skills Office, Employability Office or Job-Readiness Centre. Most, if not all, universities and colleges have one.

Some centres are centralised while others are faculty-based. This is especially true for technical degrees, with Work Integrated Learning (WIL) becoming prominent over the last few years. Find these centres as early as possible and ask about the range of services they provide.

Those services typically include:

- career planning
- cover letter review
- interview preparation
- LinkedIn headshots
- LinkedIn workshops
- resume writing.

Not bad for being a free service! So, if you want to get those employable skills and grow your career knowledge as early as possible, I suggest you find your Career Centre.

Just to clarify, I'm not saying that you should go there regularly during your first year. But you should be aware of such services early in your degree, especially when most centres help you find a casual or part-time job while you study.

So, **GROW** your knowledge about your university's Career Centre. The earlier you do this, the better it will be for your journey!

1.4.2. Your Degree

I suspect that you've already gone over your course plan and sequence of subjects during your first week. What you can do now is do that extra bit of research. Get to know everything about your studies. This includes the other faculties, courses offered, the course coordinators and course convenors.

By doing this extra bit of research, you'll know where your course or degree can lead to, particularly its potential career paths. Why is this important? It's because things will change.

The reality is your perception of your course along with its job prospects (if you've thought about those like GRAD 1 or GRAD 2 students would) will most likely change by the time you graduate. Along with the skills you acquire, this may put you on a completely different path than the one you initially planned during your first year. Yes, there will be similarities in the technical skills required between jobs in certain fields such as Engineering and Information Technology. But the technical insights and soft skills you acquire by the time you graduate are likely to change your opinion about what your *'dream job'* is.

By being involved early in your degree, you're able to make well-informed decisions. These may include changing your course, major or university later on, which will give you better control of your journey. And this is only possible by having a thorough knowledge about what options are available to you.

So, **GROW** your knowledge about your degree. The earlier you do this, the better it will be for your journey!

1.4.3. Your Colleagues

It's a known fact that the students you meet during your first year can greatly shape and impact your university life. Your colleagues form a crucial part of your network. Making and maintaining your connections pays off socially and professionally once you graduate. Naturally, you'll find yourself spending time with only a handful of them as the months pass by. That's perfectly fine. But remember how important your network is to your journey. Grow it. Make connections. There's no better time to do that than your first year. (Well, there's also the study abroad program but that's a topic for Chapter 2).

Meet as many students as you can. Connect with those from different majors, courses, campuses and even universities. Moreover, you'll also get to meet tutors and lecturers from different professional and academic backgrounds, which will exponentially grow your network. While they're not your colleagues technically, connecting with them can greatly help you in your graduate journey.

One direct benefit of networking is the fact that you get better at choosing members for group assignments. Speaking of group assignments, every student who has ever gone to university has their share of experiences with group projects, with some good while others not so much.

In fact, very few students had good groups the first time. This is especially true when you hear all the stories about students never showing up, but getting the same mark for a project as the others! My experience was not any different, as you will read in the next section.

So one thing you can do, once you feel confident with students in your course who are doing a similar sequence of subjects, is getting involved in available study groups on campus. You may not guarantee a perfect group, but you sure would have increased the chances of having good group dynamics, and made it easier to navigate such a journey with the support of your group. Not only that some of the study group members might end up in your group assignments, but more importantly, that group experience will help you acquire skills that will make you more employable!

We will speak more about teamwork in the next section and in Chapter 2. But the bottom line is this: get to know your colleagues on campus and establish quality networks so you can increase your chances of having a good experience with group projects.

So in short, **GROW** your network of colleagues and friends early on. The earlier you do this, the better it will be for your journey!

1.5 Grow Emotionally!

I want you to recall one of your first-year group assignments. What do you remember most about that group? Let me guess: that member who barely showed up and never communicated but got the same mark as you did. Frustration kicks in every time you remember that experience, doesn't it?

Do you also remember the teamwork and leadership skills you were expected to develop through that group assignment? And have you figured out how to develop those exactly? Not yet? Don't worry. I'm here to tell you how: Engage your team. Communicate. Divide the tasks amongst yourselves and deliver.

These may be easier said than done but you have to do these if you want to acquire the skills. Come to think of it, your problematic study group can help you discover and develop these. (More on this later on).

Going back to that group assignment I told you to recall, I want you to think why it unfolded the way it did. I'll take a guess. One of you didn't do their part. Let's call that person 'The Unmotivated Member'. You and your other group members told them repeatedly to do their part, but they didn't act on it. Then your grades came out. All of you got the same mark, including your unmotivated member. It seemed unfair.

How do I know this? It's because I had the same exact experience in one of my first year subjects. We had The Unmotivated Member in our group. Let's call him John (This isn't his real name, of course).

John and I were grouped with another student, Joseph. The project consisted of an assignment and a presentation, both to be delivered on Week 12.

I still remember the interesting statement our teacher made after assigning the project:

'Now that the groups have formed, I don't want anyone to come to me saying this person is not doing any work or that member shouldn't be in our group'. As someone new at group projects, I thought that his statement was a strange one.

Yet, fast-forward to a few weeks before Week 9, Joseph and I found ourselves complaining about John to our teacher.

'He cancelled every meeting we planned! We even changed the time of the meeting to suit him and he still didn't attend!' we said with visible frustration.

Our teacher reaffirmed his previous statement and replied, *'As stated in the first class, I don't want anyone to come to me saying this person is not doing any work or that member shouldn't be in our group. We are in Week 9 now, and it is unfair for that member to change his group without him being involved in the discussion.'*

'We asked him to come here. He never responded.' We uttered. It was clear that our conversation was not going anywhere. We were basically left to deal with it.

As we were preparing to leave, I couldn't help but ask the teacher, *'Do you think what's happening here is fair?'*

'Fair?...Absolutely!' He responded. *'Let me tell why this is fair. Do you think you are the first batch I teach? I have these types of issues every semester. My job is not to get too*

involved in each of the 10 groups or so, or their problems, that would be ridiculous. I am here to facilitate the conversation and establish the guidelines.'

'The reality is, you will have all kinds of challenges in the workplace. And if you can't manage this, you won't be ready to join the workforce. I know you think you've done everything. But let me tell you how I would've done it if I were you.'

Joseph and I got comfortable in our seats and paid more attention.

He said, 'From the very first class, you could have established some guidelines for the group, then referred to them. Further you would have addressed any issues with John much earlier in the semester. Let's say John is lazy and not doing his work. So, what have YOU done about it? Did you tell me in Week 3 or 4? No. You waited until the assignment was due then came to my office!'

He further added:

'Teamwork is a real skill. And the ability to act proactively and react logically with minimal emotions involved is something you should learn early. That is leadership— doing whatever it takes for the overall success of the team.'

Joseph and I left the office confused. We did the rest of the project on our own and submitted it, only for John to get the same high mark! Looking back, that was not the worst outcome, especially when I still hear how many final year group projects go horribly wrong. I'm glad I had that experience in my first year.

While I still had my share of frustrations in later group projects, I believe that having grown emotionally from that experience helped me in becoming a better group member and team player.

GROW emotionally and develop 'people skills' early in your degree. These will help you grow professionally and personally. And yes, you guessed it, the earlier you do this, the better it will be for your journey!

GROW | **ACQUIRE** | TARGET | EMBRACE

CHAPTER 2

ACQUIRE
(2nd YEAR)

Okay. Your first year honeymoon phase is over. Your so-called 'growing time' was great, as you built the foundations for your degree and overall growth. Now, it's time to let your curiosity take over. Grow your knowledge. Acquire more skills. And of course, continue to have fun.

Your second year is when you acquire most employable skills. It's also the year where some students start to have second thoughts about their degree of choice, whether it's related to what they wanted. If you're a GRAD 1, you probably won't relate to this. But if you're a GRAD 2 or GRAD 3, you may experience this type of uncertainty.

To be clear, most students continue with their first choice of course. Nevertheless, one cannot ignore the thousands who switch their major, course, or drop out of university altogether by this stage.

This phase in one's studies can truly be frustrating and disappointing. It was for me and my family. Having gone through it all, I just want you to know that there isn't a right or wrong decision. Each situation is unique. Mine was. Yours is too. But one thing is always true: You don't know what awaits once you make the decision. The closest to knowing you can get is to arm yourself with information. The more knowledge you acquire, the better and more informed your decision will be. While this doesn't allow you to see into the future, it gives you an insight to the possibilities. As a result, you become more comfortable to make the call.

There are many ways for you to spend the rest of your university days (if you decide to continue your degree). But whether you decide to continue on or make the switch, one action that is guaranteed to make you a more employable graduate is getting a job!

2.1 Get A Job!

Other than the obvious financial benefit, getting a job will help you become more employable. I strongly suggest making it your top priority (besides doing well in your studies, that is). It doesn't have to be related to your degree yet (but this would be the best case scenario). Any casual or part-time job will do. What's important is you start acquiring the basic skills that will help you in your graduate journey. If you already had a job in high school or got one in your first year studying at university, great work! That tells me that you already know the importance of it, particularly for your journey.

One easy way to find out what jobs are available is to use your network. Ask your contacts if they know anyone hiring. Another way to do this is by simply walking into a retail shop (for example) and handing in your resume to the manager. This may not be the norm now, but it shows your eagerness to work. Different methods work for different people. Either way, it may seem like a lot of effort and not all of these could pay off. But remember this: If you don't ask, the answer will always be no! If you never try, you'll never get hired.

For my part, I took on different jobs during my studies. Those included being a door-to-door salesman, kitchen hand, waiter, retail staff, Uber driver and full-time cleaner. I was a good fit for some of these roles, but performed poorly in others to the point that I was either left on my own to do the job or let go. Just imagine how that affected my confidence. Still, I'm proud and thankful that I took all of those jobs. By doing so, I found out which ones I excelled at and where I needed to improve. I realised that some roles were for me while others weren't. More importantly, the work I did helped me acquire invaluable skills, learnings and qualities that I pride myself on. These include good communication, empathy, confidence, resilience, and most importantly, people skills.

I can assure you that there are no shortages of jobs, but there can be a shortage of the willingness to do them.

So, regardless of how you find your job or what it is, working on a part-time or casual basis will set you apart from your colleagues and the graduate competition later on. You may ask yourself if this is 'worth the hassle'. The short answer: Absolutely yes! Why? Let's break it down.

2.1.1. You Will Have Experience

By the time you graduate, the majority of jobs you'll apply for will require some level of experience. While it may not be in your chosen field (in case you haven't got one by the time you graduate), the experience you have will matter. Do you remember the skills I mentioned earlier that I learnt when I took on different jobs? Those skills are crucial in your graduate search. By acquiring them and stating them on your resume, you increase your credibility, as opposed to someone who never took on a job before. Nothing says 'I am employable' more than being employed.

2.1.2. You Will Have Skills

Skills come with experience. As I mentioned in the point above, the skills you acquire while working in your casual or part-time job will prove to be essential. Such transferable skills are important in any job you decide to take. These include customer service, leadership, problem-solving, teamwork, documentation and reporting, conflict resolution and communication. This is why it doesn't matter what type of job you have right now. Just get one. Working and acquiring the necessary skills will make a significant difference in your employability. We'll talk more about transferable skills in a later section. For now, just trust me. Get a job and acquire the skills.

2.1.3. You Will Have Money

Being the most obvious benefit, having a job gives you a certain level of financial security. As such, having a basic source of income during your studies, or even after that when you are looking for a graduate job can significantly ease the pain of rejection.

Be financially independent. Your job search will be a completely different experience from a candidate who is in survival mode and is clinging to get any job opportunity. Along with its nature, the frequency of your work doesn't matter at this point. What matters (besides the employable skills) is the relative financial security that having work provides. Get employed now to get employed later!

ACQUIRE as much experience, skills and money as you can now so you have a greater possibility of getting your dream job later!

2.2 Study Abroad!

As you're now in your second year, you're most likely very familiar with your course and the university facilities. You also spend your time with your colleagues and the social groups you've made on campus. And let's not forget the work experience you've achieved so far. You've done very well! But before you get too comfortable, I want you to consider studying abroad. Yes, I am asking you to leave your newly-found comfort zone and establish a new one abroad!

What does it mean to study abroad? It means that you spend a period of time, be it a few weeks on a study tour or a whole semester in an educational institution in a foreign country. It's also called 'going on exchange' by some. Usually, it lasts for a semester or two. It can also extend longer than that depending on your university.

I can comfortably say that going abroad was the best thing that happened to me! I know it's a big statement, but a true one. By going on exchange, I experienced the best chapter of my life.

Not only did I create wonderful memories and long-lasting friendships, but I also learnt important life skills. Moreover, I was able to acquire more employable skills. Other than that (and as one would expect), I was able to create my international network.

Studying abroad is a truly life-changing experience. It will transform the way you perceive everything, from your education, job, career, friends to your very self. Ask anyone who has studied abroad, not only will they agree with me, but they'll surely talk passionately about it (just like what I'm doing right now).

It's true that there's a minority of students who didn't have a great exchange experience. I do feel bad for them. But the vast majority will tell you that it's one of the best things, if not the best thing, they have ever done in their entire lives.

To be honest, it does feel strange saying this in 2020 when travelling seems nothing but a distant memory. (Thanks COVID-19!) But when things go back to normal, however that may look, make going on exchange a priority.

By now, I hope you know the great value that studying abroad offers. I hope that you've decided to do it or even consider it. If not, what could be stopping you? Is it the thought of uncertainty and leaving your comfort zone? Believe me, I know that can be scary. Your comfort zone provides a haven. But you'll never know what lies beyond if you don't leave. You'll never know the possibilities in store if you don't take the chance. Personally, I regret not going on exchange as much as I could have. I only went twice, but could've done it three times. That's how much I believe in its benefits.

Other than the uncertainty, one main objection some have against going on exchange is how expensive it can be. To address this, let me point out three things:

1. Relatively speaking, very few countries in the world are more expensive than Australia in terms of living cost. Therefore, you'll have almost the same, if not cheaper, living expenses in any other country than you do in Australia.

2. If you're an Australian citizen and eligible, you can get an OS-HELP loan from the Australian Government. It's a one-off payment paid BEFORE you start your

semester abroad. *(As of December 2020, it's A\$ 6,913 per semester. If you study in Asia, it's A\$ 8,295.)*

3. Most universities offer scholarships for their exchange programs. These can cover a significant portion of your expenses. And did you know? Most scholarships are actually less competitive than you may think.

Now that we've addressed the objections regarding studying abroad, let's tackle the most common question students have when researching about it: What's the best destination?

Actually, the destination doesn't matter as much as you think it does. While the UK and the US are considered the most popular options for Australian students, I didn't go to either country. But both of my semesters abroad were just as good, if not better.

My first exchange was in Enschede, The Netherlands, a small city not far from the German border. And as you may have guessed, it was a great experience. To be honest, I initially thought that it was going to be boring. The place didn't seem to offer much to students, let alone international students. But was I wrong! My exchange experience was the exact opposite. There was nothing boring about it!

Then my second semester abroad I spent in Monterrey, the third largest city in Mexico. Again, while the city was a bit of an upgrade from Enschede, as it was bigger in size and there were more things to do, I didn't think it was the best city out there in terms of tourist sites. But my experience in Mexico exceeded my wildest expectations! The country was rich in culture and the people I met were really great.

During both semesters, I met people who were just like me—international students from various universities and of different nationalities who went abroad to experience something new and explore the unknown. It was the easiest time of my life to meet students, travelling buddies and best friends. Everyone was approachable and there were many events to meet new people. In fact, I stayed in touch with some of them even after the exchange. I consider them my closest friends, even closer than friends I have known for much longer in Australia. Believe me, the bond you form with exchange friends will be unparalleled, regardless of your destination!

You can always choose a destination for language, educational or cultural reasons. But even if you go on exchange just for the sake of it, that's good enough.

Before we end this section, I want to clarify another point. I know that we all have different circumstances; so going abroad may not be as easy for some as it is for others. But if you can, do it. It will give you a different perspective on life. Then along with life and employable skills, you could also learn a foreign language you never would have learnt. And most importantly, you will create lasting memories that you will cherish for life.

ACQUIRE more experiences through studying abroad now, so you have a greater possibility of getting your dream role later!

2.3 Transferable Skills

What do getting a job and studying abroad have in common? Here's a clue. They both teach what this section is all about. They both teach transferable skills. A transferable skill is any skill you can transfer (and use) from one situation to another, whether it's between countries, degrees or jobs. These could be personal, social or professional.

- **Personal:** Some of the personal skills include confidence, discipline, determination, proactiveness and resilience.

- **Professional:** Some of the professional skills include information technology, teamwork, team management, numeracy skills and research skills.

- **Social:** Some of the social skills include active listening, communication, empathy, and relationship management.

Some transferable skills fit in different categories such as adaptability, critical thinking, conflict management, flexibility, leadership, problem solving and time management.

Why are transferable skills important? It's because they are employable skills. What impact do they have in real life? Let's have a look.

What do **Arnold Schwarzenegger**, **Donald Trump** and **Dwayne *The Rock'* Johnson** have in common? Yes, they're all famous personalities. But other than that, they all have transferable skills that helped them transition from one field to another professionally without prior experience.

Take **Arnold Schwarzenegger,** for example. He's a fitness figure best known for his bodybuilding physique. He's considered as one of the greatest bodybuilders, if not the greatest, of all time. He won Mr Olympia in 1970 at the age of 23, making him the youngest ever to grab the award— a record he still holds to this day. He also went on to win the title six more times.

A few years later, he started his acting career. (We know how that turned out.) He became a very famous Hollywood icon. He's best known for his action movies, notably the Terminator franchise. *'Hasta la vista, baby'*, for example, is a catchphrase he popularised through one of those movies.

Aside from bodybuilding and acting, Arnold took on another career. He became the 38th governor of the biggest state in the US in terms of economy, California. He held the position from 2003 to 2011. Not a bad career, huh?

Next, we have **Donald Trump.** He was a businessman and television personality before becoming the 45th US president. Regardless of which side of politics you identify with, Trump's election in 2016 was a surprise to many people around the world, particularly journalists and political analysts. While I'm in no position to analyse the social, economic and political factors that contributed to the event, I know for a fact that there's something often missed when describing Trump's presidential election.

While some argue that he proved that anyone could become a president, what people often miss are the transferable skills that he accumulated over the years as a businessman and television personality— skills that made him win. In fact, Trump is the only president in the US history to get elected without any prior experience in a public office or a military background.

Then there's **Dwayne *'The Rock'* Johnson.** Before becoming an actor, he started as a wrestler. He won several championships and established his brand as *'The Rock'*. But did you know that wrestling was actually his Plan B? Initially, he aspired to become a professional football player. He played for the University of Miami and signed with a Canadian team after graduation. However, two months into training with his new team, he was cut due to injuries! As a result, he decided to return home to the US and started his wrestling career soon after.

With years of a successful career as a wrestler under his belt, he slowly made the move into acting. After starring in various roles both in film and television, Forbes magazine reported that Dwayne Johnson has become the highest-paid actor in the world in 2019. He also made Time magazine's *'100 Most Influential People'* list and was featured on one of its covers that year!

These three individuals showed such persistence in acquiring skills that they could utilise in the different fields they pursued. Before you argue that none of these men represents a typical graduate, I never said they did. I chose these men to illustrate what transferable skills can do to help you succeed in whatever career you choose.

Arming yourself with these skills will not only help you transition from one setting to another smoothly, but also help you excel in your chosen field. This is exactly what Arnold Schwarzenegger, Donald Trump and Dwayne *'The Rock'* Johnson did. They applied transferable skills like the ability to read people, entertain them and influence and shape their opinion about a certain topic. As a graduate, that's exactly what you should be doing.

Along with technical and teamwork skills, communicating, networking and presenting are all needed to a certain degree in almost any job. So how do you acquire such skills when you haven't started working in your field or have limited exposure to the workplace? There'll be many aspects to this. Let's break it down to how you can learn some transferable skills while on campus.

One of the easiest ways to do so is to join student clubs and get involved. Regardless of the size of the university you go to, you'd have a few of them on campus. Each has a different focus from academics, hobbies, sports, advocacies to culture.

Remember the O-Week that we discussed in Chapter 1? Now, it's your turn to provide that experience. It's your turn to get involved in leading the activities and show first-year students around. You might even get a chance to facilitate sessions for them by guiding and providing them with some kind of mentorship, be it academic or social. Having spent a couple of years on campus, you are more knowledgeable now than ever. Why not put it to use?

Joining students clubs and getting involved will help you acquire and polish your leadership, presentation and public speaking skills. All of these are needed in the workplace, in one way or another, regardless of which job you may have. Master these as a graduate and you will go from GRAD 3 to GRAD 2 or even GRAD 1 in no time!

ACQUIRE transferable skills now so you can transition smoothly between different fields, jobs or even careers later on. Let's start with teamwork!

2.3.1. Teamwork

Remember the story I shared in Chapter 1 about my first-year group project? Like I said then, it frustrates me every time I remember it. But I'm very thankful it happened when it did. Because I went through such an experience early in my degree, I was able to learn and improve myself as a group member. I gained better teamwork skills.

During your studies, you'll be grouped with different students whom you may or may not necessarily like. Here's a fact: You don't have to be friends with your teammates for all of you to work well together. You don't have to get along with them on a personal level. In contrast to that, you will not always have the best dynamics when you work with friends. You will not always get the best outcome. Believe me. As ugly as it may sound, this is true. Friendship is not an employable skill. Teamwork is! That's why you should practice it along with professionalism during your studies. It goes without saying that these skills will be expected of you once you enter the workforce. Let me tell you a story to further illustrate my point.

In one of my second-year business classes, the teacher asked us to form groups for our group assignment. As I didn't know anyone in the class, I stood with a few others in a corner as per the teacher's instructions. (I know this sounds like a punishment, but that was just the process.) Then, she divided us into our respective groups of four members each.

Afterwards, she explained why she found group projects interesting. On one hand, she said that some of the groups she taught previously had members who didn't know each other beforehand. But they worked well as a team and got an exceptionally high mark at the end of the semester. However, they didn't stay in touch after. On the other hand, she also mentioned a couple of cases where group members didn't know each other as well and didn't perform the best. But they ended up becoming best friends after the semester. After hearing that, I remember thinking to myself, *'How can students work together so well without developing a good personal relationship?'*

Ironically, that's what happened with our group at the end of that semester! We managed to deliver one of the best group projects, but we didn't stay in touch after that. Did we dislike each other? No, not at all. We had a great time and got along really well. We even had a few drinks after our final presentation to celebrate. We just didn't see any reason to continue the relationship on a personal level.

In teams, the overall success doesn't depend on how good of a friendship you have with each other. Rather, it hinges on the project scope, team mission and cooperation. As for our group, we understood our mission and worked accordingly. And that's what teamwork is all about.

As you've read in Chapter 1 under "Grow Emotionally!", you'd know that teamwork wasn't always my strongest suit. But as one evolves and does more group work, they become a better team player, which is the case for most second-year and third-year students.

So, **ACQUIRE** and improve your teamwork skills by getting involved. Take part in both individual and group projects such as assignments and presentations.

2.3.2. Presentations

Ah, presentations! If you get overwhelmed with fear by the mere thought of doing one, I'm here to assure you that what you're feeling is normal. It even has a medical term *'Glossophobia'*, which is the fear of public speaking. It is estimated to affect 75% of the population! While most people experience it on some level, some people just practise and get better at managing it. Moreover, being confident as a person doesn't always guarantee delivering a great presentation. Similarly, being an introvert doesn't equate to presenting badly.

Speaking of being an introvert, I'd like to clarify something while we're at it. It's not the same as being shy. Yes, they are different. An introvert enjoys time alone and gets emotionally drained after spending a lot of time with others. A shy person doesn't necessarily want to be alone, but is afraid to interact with others. And while I was both shy and introvert in first year of uni, I now consider myself an introvert, but not shy.

You can be the biggest introvert, but also be the most confident speaker and presenter. Similarly, you can be an extrovert, but get your audience lost and confused with an information overload, especially if your presentation doesn't have a clear structure. Having clarified those, I want you to know that the ability to deliver presentations well is a skill you can learn. Yes, it's true that some people naturally have it. But this doesn't mean that you can't be the same. After all, having good presentation skills is something expected of you whether you're a student or a professional.

The context of conducting presentations varies. But as a student, one clear opportunity for you to practice it is through group presentations.

Let's take a trip down memory lane again. In one of my first-year subjects, we had to present for 30 minutes as a group of five members. Some of us were more comfortable doing it than others. So, we decided to divide the time accordingly. Those members who were less comfortable only presented one slide each towards the end. As a group, we felt like we did a great job and merited a high, if not a full mark. Oh, how wrong we were! The teacher didn't share our opinion. We barely passed. He also gave us feedback about our performance. It was probably the most structured and detailed assessment anyone could get about a presentation. (Well, it was for me.) I have summarised his four points below and added my input.

1. In reference to the overall flow of our presentation, the teacher said that there was a clear disconnect with the audience due to an inconsistency in our voice projection. Some of us spoke clearly and confidently while others presented softly in a narrating voice.

2. He said that some of us presented with a confident approach and only took a few glances on the slides while others chose to read from their notes. NEVER read from your notes. I know this is a scary thought, but remember that the audience doesn't know the exact flow or content of your presentation. Deviating from your script and being natural on how you execute your flow makes for a much better delivery than reading from your notes.

3. Further to the previous point, he said that our use of body language and eye contact was limited. This was

because we were consciously thinking about just finishing the slide and sticking to the time limit. It was clear that the audience was disengaged towards the end of the presentation.

4. Finally, he said that our allocation of time per member should be close to equal. Rightly so, since the only way to improve your presentation skills is to actually get enough time to present.

As you might've guessed, my group and I only met for a few minutes before we did our actual presentation in front of the class. We didn't rehearse at all. So from there on, I got into the habit of rehearsing the subsequent presentations in full, at least once.

Speaking of rehearsing, there are many ways to improve your presentation skills. Some of these are recording yourself, presenting to someone or talking in front of a mirror. Through these, you can gauge how knowledgeable you are about the topic at hand. You'll also determine how natural you sound and make your ideas flow together without exceeding the allotted time if any. Remember that just like with any other skill, practice makes perfect when it comes to presentation.

To **ACQUIRE** great presentation skills, keep practising. Keep training to keep improving.

2.3.3. Communication

Communication is integral to both teamwork and presentation skills. It can be expressed in different ways. Some of these are body language, tone of voice, calls, graphs, emails, emojis, letters, memes, social media, reports, texts, videos and voice notes.

The more you understand a situation and communicate accordingly, the more employable you become. To that point, the better your communications skills are, the better you get at networking and the more likely you are to secure a job.

To stay within the scope of this book, let's focus on the main type of communication you'll encounter during your studies along with ways on how to improve it: **Written Communication**.

Written Communication is probably one of the most underrated employable skills. There isn't much focus on it unless your degree or job revolves around it. We're here to change that. To start, read and compare the following statements.

Statement 1:

'It has been widely noted by academics and business leaders alike that the consensus achieved in Australia at the state and federal levels has appropriately addressed the unprecedented challenge that COVID-19 posed on the economy.'

Statement 2:

'Everyone thinks that Australian politicians agreeing on the coronavirus solutions is good for the economy.'

Both of the statements above convey a similar message. But which one are you likely to use in a formal report? How about in a quick email or text?

The tone and words you use to communicate should change depending on the context. Have you ever been misunderstood over a text? Or how about doing your best in writing an email only to be told it was too formal or too friendly? If either of these has happened to you, you're not alone! We've all been there. The only way to improve your writing skills is to keep writing. Write more reports to become better at it. Create more emails to come up with better quality output.

To stay within the scope of this book, let's focus on formal and professional written communication. Perhaps one of the most important forms, if not the most important form, of this type of communication is **email writing.** Since not all emails are written in the same context, there isn't a strict set of rules for creating one. But here are a few tips:

A. **Say 'Dear' instead of 'Hi'.** Whenever you're unsure whether to use 'Hi' as the starting line or greeting of your email, use 'Dear'. If the recipient responds with a 'Hi', then you can reply accordingly. Don't use informal or casual language to communicate with someone via email unless they initiate it, especially if you haven't met each other yet.

B. **Keep it short and simple (KISS).** Be concise. Regardless of the purpose of your email, whether it's a request for an assignment extension or an enquiry about alternative sessions, your recipient shouldn't have to go through four or five paragraphs to figure out what you want. Greet, get to the point and finish. The subject of your email should also be short and specific.

Professors, recruiters, and directors get tens, if not hundreds, of emails daily. So, the quicker you get to the point, the easier it is for them to understand and attend to your request.

C. **Make the subject clear**. As I mentioned in the previous point, the subject of your email should be short and specific. Given that your email may be one of the hundreds a person receives in a day, its title or the subject field should be as clear as possible. Are you asking for advice? Are you looking for an extension? Is it an urgent matter? If your subject isn't clear, the recipient may not prioritise it. So, make sure your subject is specific and says what your email is all about.

D. **Review before sending**. Do yourself a favour and fully read your email before hitting '*Send*'. You may discover that the language you used is too direct or slightly aggressive. Inversely, you may realise that your email actually sounds vague or that you haven't said everything you wanted to say. Reviewing your email also allows you to correct any spelling errors you may have missed. So, make it a habit to read through your email before sending it. It will only take a few minutes of your time at most and save you from potential embarrassment later.

E. **Always be nice.** There'll be instances when someone will not respond to your email within the time you expect. Naturally, you'll send a follow-up email or two. When you still get no response, you may feel inclined to send a strongly-worded email to prompt them to reply. DON'T! Be careful not to sound offensive or rude in any of your emails. It could only complicate things. It also doesn't add any value to your case. If anything, it damages your reputation, negatively affects your emotions and ruins someone else's day.

While it is easy to assume that the recipients of your email are ignoring you on purpose, there are other reasons why they are not responding. These include them forgetting about your email, preferring a different method of communication or having much-higher priorities. Regardless of the reason, always ensure that you remain polite and professional.

All right. So, now that you can communicate, present and work well with people, what do you do next? You put your skills to use and **ACQUIRE** more connections!

2.4 Network, Network, Network!

Now that you have acquired such great skills, let's put them into action. In Chapter 1, we discussed the opportunities and ways to expand your network during your first year. But now that you're in your prime university years, it's a different story.

Next to studying abroad, there are very few places on earth that offer you access to a huge network as your university does. By being proactive on campus, you can establish a network of friends and acquaintances that will benefit you for years to come.

As you network on campus, you must have a goal beyond merely acquiring new connections. You should remember that both quantity and quality connections matter.

2.4.1. Quantity

To meet as many people as you can, you'll have to be where people are! Find campus events that interest you and get involved. These can vary from leadership conferences to sporting events. As a starting point, approach any of the following groups:

- external, off-campus groups (such as cultural or religious groups)
- social groups (like the ones behind O-Week and university parties)
- study groups (like the ones you join for group assignments, the programming club or the Maths Learning Centre).

By joining on-campus and off-campus events, you can meet tens, if not hundreds, of students.

Personally, I always found politics and debates quite enjoyable. That's why I got involved with a few Model United Nations (MUN) conferences. As the name suggests, it's like the United Nations in a way. It's an educational simulation wherein you act as a delegate. As a delegate, you represent a country in a UN Agency such as the Security Council. You debate with other delegates about the issues at hand. Just like in the real UN, you draft and pass legislation by the majority of votes.

The great thing about such a concept is that you don't always have the final say in which country you represent. You could be a believer of communism but have to speak for the US or be a hardcore capitalist but assigned to represent North Korea! You're expected to do your best in presenting your party even while in unfamiliar and uncomfortable situations.

Due to the nature of MUN, I was able to improve my skills in many areas such as negotiation, public speaking, diplomacy and, most importantly, empathy. However, I believe my biggest takeaway from the MUN conferences I participated in was the networking. I had the chance to meet students from many other Australian and international universities. I even got to meet academics and politicians who participated as facilitators and speakers.

In fact, I loved my first MUN conference so much that I wrote a lengthy proposal for my university to sponsor me in an interstate MUN conference. To show its value, I outlined the benefits in terms of increasing my employability. I also stated my commitment to promoting similar opportunities by volunteering once I'm back on campus. Several emails and weeks later, my application was successful! I had the opportunity to participate in the conference and network with over 500 delegates.

Now, how does my story relate to quantity in networking? By being proactive, I was able to connect with more people than I would have otherwise.

So, **ACQUIRE** more connections by getting involved and joining on-campus and off-campus events. Not only will you expand your network, but you can also end up meeting people you never thought you would.

2.4.2. Quality

What's great about establishing your network is that it gives you the opportunity to create a good support system as well. Other than that, you can get tasks done in an efficient way through collaboration. This is true for both personal and professional connections.

But be careful not to focus solely on acquiring as many connections as you can. Remember that along with quantity, quality matters. To truly create a good support system within your network, you must work towards nurturing your connections. On the contrary, the quality of your network will deteriorate if you're only focused on the number of people you know.

For example, think of a person you haven't spoken to in years. Chances are you haven't thought of them until now, let alone reached out to them. They will also not be on the top of your list of people to contact for a favour, either due to indifference or hesitation. This creates one weak connection within your network.

So how do you establish quality connections within your network? Here are some of my personal tips to do just that.

A. Check in

Reach out to your connections. Every now and then, give them a quick call or send a simple message to know how they're doing when you can. I know it sounds simple. Yet, it's surprising how many people forget to do this. Even saying hi through a mutual friend goes a long way in reminding someone that you're thinking of them.

While you should aim to do this regularly, it's even more important to do so in times of crisis. If you think that someone you know may have been affected by an unfortunate event like a natural disaster or an accident, reach out. It's also common courtesy. Take the time out of your day to check in on them and their loved ones. This shows that you genuinely care. Moreover, gestures like this are what establishes a quality network. Once you have that, you can connect with them on a deeper level in the future.

There's no doubt that COVID-19 has been an unwelcomed surprise to many, if not all of us. But one of the good things that came out of it is the ability to connect with anyone within your network without prior context. In my case, I've had people whom I haven't spoken to in years checking in on me and my loved ones and wishing us well. Similarly, I've made the effort to reach out to many people in my network, whether through video and phone calls or direct messages on social media.

My messages read along the following lines:

'Hey, John. It's been a while I know, but I just wanted to check in on you. I heard the news about Victoria. I hope you and your family are safe and well.'

Writing and sending each message only took me around a minute, but it ended years of disconnection and revived a relationship! In many cases, it even led to hours of video call with the person and we would reconnect after years of disconnection.

B. Celebrate with them

Celebrate wins and special occasions with your connections, whether they're friends or new acquaintances. I admit I may not be the best at staying in touch with many people. But I do my best to send people good wishes on their special occasions. Be it a graduation, marriage, promotion, Christmas, having a baby, getting a new car or any other occasion worth celebrating.

Again, the good thing about such occasions is that they require no prior context. No need for awkward messages saying, *'Hey, I know we haven't spoken in years but blah, blah, blah.'* The occasions create the context and congratulating them on their success is always welcomed and appreciated.

C. Happy Birthday!

Technically, birthdays are still considered celebrations. But for some reason, they hit differently. There's such an inexplicable great feeling when someone greets you during your birthday, especially when their greeting is unexpected. We all know that feeling. In fact, you just recalled one, didn't you? So what's your job here? Be that someone!

In my case, I try my best to send a personalised birthday message. I do this either through a call or a written message when I can't greet them in person. Depending on how long I've known the person, I either remind them of a previous interaction we had or tell them how great they are and how blessed I am to have them in my network.

When it comes to written messages like SMS and via social media, I also make use of emojis (usually faces) showing different emotions. I believe adding celebratory and happy emojis conveys a great deal of enthusiasm and excitement, much more than a plain text would.

Other than sending a written message, you may also want to call certain people. I also use voice notes for such occasions, as I find them personal enough without disturbing the person or greeting them at the wrong time.

ACQUIRE quality connections by reaching out and staying in touch. And remember to be genuine about it.

2.5 Social Media

Now, let's talk about social media. If you're reading this book, you're most likely a student or a graduate who's well versed in it. If my guess is right, you have accounts on all platforms from Instagram to TikTok. (Well, you're on either all or most of them.) While we're on the subject, I suggest you create one on LinkedIn if you still haven't. I will discuss why and talk about this platform in detail in Chapter 3. But for now, believe me when I say that it's vital to your graduate journey.

So, why are we discussing social media? It's because it's important in networking.

To be honest, I did have a phase during my university studies when I deleted ALL of my social media accounts. I didn't have any for over a year! While my move supports arguments to reduce social media use or disable it during examination periods, it was still a wrong move.

Even if it also addressed my concerns on privacy, I missed out on so many networking opportunities. I also didn't have a television at that time so my only source of news and information was word of mouth!

I remember when I got back on social media, I caught up on a lot of stuff including hundreds of memes! Along with other social topics, it was great to connect with people on something light and funny. I see it as a laid-back type of networking. No fuss. However, while that was fun, what wasn't is the fact that I lost a lot of opportunities to connect with people while on hiatus.

To be clear, I'm not saying that you should be glued to your accounts all day. I just want you to understand its importance in networking. Social media is already integrated into our daily lives, whether we like it or not. Companies use it to hire employees. Professionals use it to connect. Do the same and be wise about it.

So, get social! **ACQUIRE** more connections and nurture existing ones by using social media platforms.

2.6 International Students

Before I conclude this chapter of acquiring skills and delve into how to approach jobs, I would like to draw attention to a large and vital segment of the student population in Australia: **International students.**

According to the 2018 Australian Government (pre-COVID) statistics, there are nearly 800,000 international students in Australia. It is no secret that international students and graduates face greater challenges in finding full-time employment in Australia. Yes, the odds might be stacked against you as an international student, but you should not put limits on yourself.

There is no doubt that one of those employability challenges is the visa. As the Australian Immigration rules and regulations change quite often, and each student case is different, I am in no position to offer advice here. Address the legal aspect with your agency or trusted immigration lawyer, and do your research to ensure you have the latest advice, as it can change at short notice.

Now, let's talk about what makes you unique as an international student, so you can turn such challenges into success stories, just like the professionals interviewed in Chapter 4 did.

Start thinking about all the transferable skills and qualities that you acquired in your studies and lifestyle changes, which make you unique as an international student, and present yourself as such to employers.

Let me help you - here are some:

A. **Adaptability:** As an international student, by definition, you have had to adapt to living in another country. This means a different culture, way of thinking and living conditions altogether. You are already studying abroad, so regardless of how much travelling you have done during your studies, you already have become more adaptable than someone who has not studied abroad. Make sure you use such a skill to your advantage, especially when presenting yourself to an employer. To add to that point, being adaptable means that you are more likely (and willing) to relocate for the job, and this very fact makes you more employable.

B. **Community:** Following up on the previous point, and reversing the roles, one tends to forget the very uniting factor of identity. This is evident in the people you hang around with as an international student, with some, if not most of them, being from your home country or region. Use such a support network to your advantage, personally and professionally.

C. **Experience:** Whether you are trying to find full-time employment in Australia to stay, or just get your degree and go back to your home country, consider this opportunity to study abroad as a great personal experience. This will undoubtedly serve you well in the future, both personally and professionally. Ensure you cherish and celebrate such a journey.

D. **Independence:** Since you chose to study in a foreign country (Australia in this case), you have decided to take matters into your own hands. The very skill of independence means that you have managed not only your daily responsibilities such as cooking, laundry and personal finance, but also other major life decisions such as studies, work and relationships. While not having your familiar surroundings such as family and friends in your home country was initially a disadvantage, the bright side is that it fuelled your hunger to seek more opportunities in the new environment. Being independent means that you can be proactive about your employability much earlier in your degree.

E. **Perspective:** As someone who has lived in different cultures and had double the exposure, you are sure to have a certain perspective about what a good job is, or how to find one. Make sure you use your perspective to your advantage. For example, I know of countless international groups on Facebook that are based solely on that idea, as they help each other in finding hacks and ways to get both casual and professional employment.

In short, **ACQUIRE** your unique selling points as an international student, and present yourself accordingly to the future employers.

GATE

GROW | ACQUIRE | **TARGET** | EMBRACE

CHAPTER 3
TARGET
(FINAL YEAR)

In the past two chapters, we have covered ways for you to grow and acquire the knowledge and skills that make you more employable. Now, you are approaching your graduation in your final year, or you have already graduated, and just want to find a job.

Since we spoke quite a bit about networking and transferable skills, it only makes sense to apply for jobs now. You are here, you are about to graduate, and you don't have a job. You might experience panic attacks, frustration and lack of purpose as a graduate, which is definitely not fun. But the good news is that you can avoid such feelings by approaching your job search with strategy and logic, so let's get jobs!

3.1 Let's Get Jobs!

'Do I need a Cover Letter? Should I add my casual job to my resume? What about volunteering? Do all companies have assessment centres? How am I supposed to get experience when no one wants to hire me without having it in the first place? Can I get a job with my average marks?'

You've probably heard such questions or even asked them yourself in the past. I know I did. When I was approaching my final year, I returned from my second exchange, and since I deferred my degree to travel, I frankly didn't know anyone on campus upon returning.

Besides some casual jobs, I didn't exactly have work experience in the field of business, be it accounting, finance, human resources or any business-related expertise. Further, I didn't have the best grades either (not that I am proud of it, I am just stating the facts). What made things even worse was that I had no idea what I wanted to do in life, let alone finding a job.

As you already read in the introduction of this book, I was lost, so lost! Yes, the process of finding a job can be daunting and frustrating, but it doesn't have to be. After months of learning about the job market and finally securing a graduate role, coupled with a few years of working for the Big-4 consulting firms, let me tell you that you will be ok!

While we're here, and as management consulting and the Big-4 seem to be hot topics for most business graduates, let's address them first. Then, we will look at some job finding tips, in order to bypass most of the unnecessary frustrations.

3.2 Management Consulting & The Big-4

When I was at university, I always thought that people who worked for the Big-4 firms were from a different planet, exceptionally competent and have skills that are unattainable by the rest of us. While there is some truth to the incredible talent there, a lot of graduates today mistakenly think it's nearly impossible to get a role in the Big-4. For reference, the Big-4 consulting firms are **Deloitte**, **EY**, **KPMG**, and **PwC**. Further, strategy consulting firms **McKinsey & Company**, **Boston Consulting Group**, and **Bain & Company** are considered the 'Big Three', or 'MBB'.

While the recruitment process for such firms can be lengthy and competitive, it is not impossible to get in. Even if you do not know anyone who works there, you should still give it a shot. Be proactive, articulate your relevant transferable skills that we discussed in Chapter 2, then apply and persevere through the interview process. You must believe that you have a chance of securing a graduate role, and you will. How do I know? Because that was me some years ago.

I certainly do not think that I was an exceptional graduate, but what I did is I prepared thoroughly, gave it my best shot, and believed that I was good enough. While I got rejected from all the Big-4 in the first round, I was able to secure a mid-year graduate role with Deloitte.

But before you only focus on working with the Big-4 as a graduate, I want you to ask yourself, *'Why do I want to work for the Big-4?'* Is it the career progression? The networking opportunities? The skills taught there? The international exposure? The brand name? Whatever your reason is, barring the fact that the Big-4 are actually "THE BIG-4" (i.e., the brand name), all of the other aspects can be addressed with other employers who provide graduates with a similar experience.

To be clear, I am not asking you not to apply for the Big-4, I am merely asking you to broaden the scope of your job search. If the Big-4 is your ultimate goal, remember that missing out on internships and graduate programs is not the end of the world. Do not be discouraged, as there are tens if not hundreds of management consulting firms out there. You have a whole career ahead of you, and there will be several opportunities for you to join as a lateral hire.

What other consulting firms are there, you may ask? Well, below is a compiled list of selected global consulting / advisory firms (in various fields) that accept graduates in Australia. These firms have some office presence in most, if not all of Australian capital cities:

1. Accenture
2. AlixPartners
3. AON Consulting
4. BDO
5. BearingPoint
6. Capgemini
7. CGI
8. Corporate Value Associates
9. Everest Group
10. Findex
11. FTI Consulting
12. Grant Thornton
13. HLB Mann Judd
14. Kearney
15. Korn Ferry
16. L.E.K. Consulting
17. Mercer
18. Milliman
19. Oliver Wyman
20. Partners In Performance
21. Pitcher Partners
22. PKF
23. Protiviti
24. RSM
25. Simon Kucher & Partners
26. William Buck

Let's fast-forward here and assume that you just started working as a graduate in one of those firms. You probably want to know what you're getting yourself into. *'What do consultants do in their job?'*. If you ask a consultant this question, you might get the vague *'Every day is different'* or *'It depends'*, only to keep wondering what those responses actually mean.

As a matter of fact, as a former consultant myself, I was asked the same question a few years ago. It was an after-hours dinner with the team, along with some external friends. A colleague's friend asked us, *'So, what do you guys actually do?'* We all looked at each other, trying to come up with an answer. After some awkward silence, I said, *'We add value!'* Although we laughed it off, that was our best answer collectively as a team, to what we've been doing for years!

After a bit of reflection, I believe a good way to summarise your role in management consulting is the following three steps:

1. **Input:** You get the information from the client about a problem or the present situation.

2. **Verification:** You validate and confirm the data or information by doing the necessary checks.

3. **Output:** You present your suggested solutions or findings to the client.

While this might be an oversimplification, almost all consulting projects follow this process in one way or another, be it in business consulting, financial consulting, human resources consulting, risk consulting, technology consulting...etc. You are essentially finding solutions to clients' problems.

Problem-solving and other transferable skills such as communication become particularly relevant here, and so do technical skills such as the competent use of Microsoft Word, Excel and PowerPoint.

While on the topic, it is worth mentioning that the graduate recruitment process differs between the Big-4 firms themselves. Nevertheless, it usually consists of online tests, assessment centres and a couple of interviews. I will speak more about the interview preparation later in this chapter.

Without going into detail about the online tests, they usually range between logical deduction, analytical and numerical tests. As a candidate, there is nothing major you can do before the online tests that will significantly change the outcome. Assuming you are in a quiet place and have a reliable connection when you start them, my advice would be to keep an eye on the time allocated, as graduates are often surprised with the lack of it towards the end.

By the same token, there is no need to overprepare for assessment centres. They often consist of a business case, which is usually a client's problem you have to solve. As you are being assessed as part of a group, skills like teamwork, communication and presentation are particularly important here.

Now that we've addressed the specific topic of management consulting, let's broaden our scope and discuss some job finding tips for the wider market.

3.3 Job Finding Tips

Whether you are after a graduate role in the Big-4, other consulting roles or any entry-level job, there are some actions you can take to make such process a smooth one.

Here are ten tips you can apply to get you there:

1. **Believe In Yourself**

   Believe that you can do it and you will! Tell yourself that you will do whatever it takes, to get your dream job. If you believe in the Law Of Attraction, you will get the job. Or you can try another proven belief, which is the placebo effect. So, placebo your way to the job!

   Come to think of it, if you don't believe that you are worthy and capable of getting a job, how do you expect an employer to believe in you? Throw out your excuses and believe in yourself!

2. **Be Loud**

   There is absolutely no shame in telling your network, be it friends, family, colleagues, or professionals in the industry that you are looking for a job. Of course, do not bring it up every single time you meet someone, as that will be just annoying! But if people in your network do not know that you are looking for a job, then you are not serious about your job search. The Business Insider estimates that at least 70% of all jobs are not advertised! Word-of-mouth is a thing, so be proactive and find those jobs by being loud!

3. Be Selective

This chapter is titled 'TARGET' for a reason. Do not waste your energy on hundreds of job applications. Do not spray and pray. So, instead of submitting low quality applications for a hundred jobs a week, for example, target ten jobs or fewer weekly with high-quality applications. Remember to track your applications (could be in an Excel spreadsheet) so you can consistently follow up and improve your approach. There are currently thousands of graduates who are not selective. (i.e. they are spraying and praying only to get frustrated with the results.) Do not be one of them.

I will talk more about the quality of applications in terms of Resumes, Cover Letters and LinkedIn in the next sections. But I know for a fact that spraying multiple low-quality job applications, and simply praying that they get something doesn't work. How do I know that? Because that is how I did NOT get a job with my initial 100 or so applications.

4. Expand Your Search

Let's assume you have already asked your network and applied for your companies of choice, then where else are you going to search? Let me help you: Google! Of course you already know how to Google things, that's what you've been doing for years. But let me suggest you some terms to Google:

'Business graduate roles Adelaide; IT entry-level jobs Sydney; Data analytics company Melbourne; 2021 graduate programme Australia; Accounting paid internship Perth; Mining engineering company

Brisbane; List of consulting companies Darwin; Automation analyst Canberra; Marketing internship sports Hobart... etc.'

Those are only suggestions, but the more you mix the terms based on your industry and geography, the closer you will get to jobs of relevance to you. By searching such terms, you will hear of job titles and companies in your field that you never knew existed.

That being said, there are known websites for job seekers in Australia, where you can start your job search. These include:

- Adzuna
- CareerOne
- GlassDoor
- GradConnection

- GumTree
- Indeed
- **LinkedIn**
- **Seek**

While Seek and LinkedIn have the widest spread overall, the other platforms have different relevance to you as a graduate depending on your industry. Nevertheless, with over 11 million Australians using LinkedIn, this platform should be your prime focus.

5. Get LinkedIn

You cannot be serious about expanding your job search without being on LinkedIn. In short, it is estimated that 95% of recruiters use LinkedIn as a primary sourcing tool to find candidates!

You can try all the other platforms mentioned earlier, but if you had to choose one platform to focus on, go all-in for LinkedIn. If you do not know where to start, refer to the LinkedIn section later in this chapter.

6. Get Social

One way to increase your chances of finding a job is to get social. I am not referring to just being social on campus with your friends, but rather you should get involved with conferences and networking events off-campus. More connections will mean more chances of finding a job.

You will see in Chapter 4 how one of the professionals interviewed did not apply for a single job! What he did instead was being proactive in socialising and participating in events, which in turn made him find several jobs through the network he created as a student.

On that note, let me tell you that transitioning to the 9-to-5 job lifestyle will be the most significant change for you, from a social point of view. Remember to enjoy your time at university as much as you can, because trust me, you will miss what you have now.

7. Go To Job Fairs

Throughout the year, you will hear of job fairs or expos where company recruiters visit your campus to find graduates and answer their questions. Do attend all of them! There are two direct benefits when you do that.

First, you will know what sort of graduate roles are out there, what kind of skills companies expect and what the deadlines are for such roles. More importantly, you will be able to directly connect with the companies' managers and recruiters, giving you a competitive advantage for future graduate applications.

8. Learn More

Chances are you've already spent hours checking memes or cute cat videos. While you're still online, I encourage you to look for short courses that relate to your field, so you can upskill accordingly. Sites like Coursera, LinkedIn Learning, Udemy, and YouTube are all great resources.

Further to that, I would like to single out one particular skill. You may have already written long reports and presented the findings using Microsoft Word and PowerPoint during your studies, but you probably haven't done a great deal of work on **Microsoft Excel.** The reliance on Excel in the industry has increased significantly in recent years. I would not exaggerate if I said that more than 30% of my workday at previous consulting roles relied on Excel data. You certainly do not have to be an Excel guru, but the ability to input, verify and analyse data from Excel is one of the biggest employable skills. Learn it now and make your life easier.

9. Remember Small Businesses

If you are anything like me as a graduate, you will most likely be looking to work for a large company, preferably an international one. However, by only looking for jobs in such companies, you are ignoring a big part of the Australian job market, which is small businesses.

According to the Australian Bureau of Statistics (ABS), small businesses (employing less than 20 people) account for almost 98% of businesses in Australia. Hence, by limiting yourself to large companies, not only are you competing with thousands of graduates, but you're also only applying to the 2%!

Working at a small business will give you great exposure and transferable skills. Granted, roles in these businesses are more challenging to find (due to the limited resources there). But once you find an opening, it is a relatively straightforward process to get hired, especially when you are competing with a few or no other candidates.

10. Visit The Career Centre (Again)

Remember the Career Centre I didn't know existed until my final year? Well, you cannot use the same excuse, since you know about such services now. Refer to Chapter 1 for more information about how they can help you. Do yourself a favour and pay them a visit. It will save you hours of unnecessary work on your job applications, just like it saved me in the final year.

3.4 Resumes

First things first, remember that 'Resume' and 'CV' (Curriculum Vitae) are used interchangeably in the real world. Although they might have slight differences in use in some contexts, they mean the same thing in Australia, at least for this context.

By this stage, it is clear that finding a job is a lot more than having a good resume. Although the resume is not your only selling document, it is still a key piece of the employment puzzle that you will have to address, and address well.

There are hundreds of templates and ways in which you can present your experience in a resume, and giving detailed advice will depend on the individual circumstances of the applicant. So, instead of showing you how to write a tailored resume, which may or may not be relevant to your circumstances, I will provide you with some practical resume tips.

Based on the common mistakes I have found by reviewing hundreds of graduate resumes, I'm hoping to equip you with the knowledge of what to include, and what not to include there. Let's start with some resume DOs & DON'Ts.

3.4.1. Resume DOs & DON'Ts

#	DO	DON'T
1	Include your name clearly on top with your contact details.	Include personal information such as your date of birth, your full address or your marital status.
2	Have your LinkedIn and hyperlink it to your name.	Have the full LinkedIn URL, just the word "LinkedIn" should do.
3	Have your contact details visible, preferably on top of your resume.	Include a photo of yourself (unless you are in an industry that requires it).
4	Have a section for the career objective / profile summary.	Only say looking for a job there, mention your relevant skills and experience to the job sought.
5	Have the education separated as its own section. You may also call it "Qualifications".	Fill this section with too many qualifications or certificates that are not relevant for the role.
6	Have your work experience in a separate section, clearly labelled as "Employment", "Work History" or "Experience".	Add more than three roles as a graduate (unless you absolutely have to); only include the roles that are relevant to what you are applying for.
7	Describe your responsibilities using clear and concise language.	List your responsibilities in two or three words each, as such are incomplete statements.
8	Quantify your responsibilities and achievements (i.e. add numbers to them).	Excessively add numbers; only quantify where relevant and appropriate.

#	DO	DON'T
9	Include additional involvement such as volunteering projects or relevant initiatives you were involved in.	Fill a whole page or two of such projects detailing every single project you have done.
10	Include transferable skills that are relevant for the role, be it technical or soft skills.	Say you are a beginner in something; you can either learn the skill / software added, or take it out if you are not comfortable including it.

Remember to keep the information factual in your resume (i.e. do not lie or make up non-existing roles). With your life experiences and skills, you are already more employable than you think!

3.4.2. Resume Action-Based Verbs

One major area of improvement I see in a lot of resumes is the repetitive use of common verbs to describe past roles, such as 'assisted', 'coordinated' and 'helped'. For a higher impact, use more powerful action-based verbs. Here is a list of 75 verbs with such impact:

1. Accelerated
2. Accomplished
3. Achieved
4. Advanced
5. Advised
6. Analysed
7. Briefed
8. Built
9. Capitalised
10. Captured
11. Collaborated
12. Constructed
13. Consulted
14. Conveyed
15. Created
16. Delivered
17. Derived
18. Designed
19. Diagnosed
20. Directed
21. Drafted
22. Drove
23. Earned
24. Edited
25. Enhanced
26. Established
27. Exceeded
28. Executed
29. Expanded
30. Finalised
31. Forecasted
32. Founded
33. Guided
34. Handled
35. Headed
36. Implemented
37. Improved
38. Increased
39. Initiated
40. Integrated
41. Investigated
42. Launched
43. Managed
44. Maximised
45. Mentored
46. Negotiated
47. Optimised
48. Oversaw
49. Partnered
50. Performed
51. Planned
52. Presented
53. Produced
54. Provided
55. Published
56. Reached
57. Reduced
58. Researched
59. Resolved
60. Reviewed
61. Secured
62. Sharpened
63. Sparked
64. Spearheaded
65. Steered
66. Stimulated
67. Strategised
68. Supervised
69. Surpassed
70. Tracked
71. Trained
72. Transformed
73. Upgraded
74. Verified
75. Won

3.4.3. The Three 'R's

Once you have compiled all the information in one updated resume, run it through *The Three 'R's* test to ensure it is **Relevant**, **Readable** and **Reviewed**. If your resume satisfies one or two R's, it will not stand out in a pile of resumes. Check that your resume passes *The Three 'R's* test before you submit it. Otherwise, you may find the job search more challenging than it should. Let's take them one by one.

A. Relevant

When writing or updating your resume, only include the positions and skills that are relevant to the role you are targeting. To be specific, I want you first to have a resume that lists every single job you have ever done, be it casual, volunteering, community work or internships. Then, add all of your skills and qualifications such as online courses, certificates and degrees. This information should make your **"Master Resume"**.

Your Master Resume is to have everything you've ever done that makes you employable. It can stretch up to four or five pages. You will never apply to any position with this resume, but it acts as a strong base for you to tailor your resume to the targeted job.

For example, if you are applying for a kitchen hand or a waiter, and a whole page of your resume talks about your law degree and internship experience, the resume is irrelevant to the restaurant. Instead, in this case, you need to include any hospitality or customer experience you have.

This also works the other way around. For a graduate role, if you have done an internship or some work experience that is related to your degree, there is no reason for you to overflow the resume with the other irrelevant hospitality and retail roles. Only focus on what is relevant to the role.

However, if you have just graduated and do not have any work experience in your field, then by all means, add your hospitality and retail jobs, or any casual jobs you've done. This is because the transferable skills from such roles make your experience relevant, as we have discussed in Chapter 2.

Furthermore, your food handling certificate or Responsible Service of Alcohol (RSA), for example, are not relevant to most jobs outside of hospitality, so do not include them if the job is an office-based one, as such irrelevant inclusion will often confuse the employer.

Because the goal of your graduate resume is to be relevant to the targeted job, the tailored resume should not be more than two pages. In most cases, you can squeeze everything in a nicely-formatted one-page resume. As a graduate with less than 2 years of work experience, if your resume is more than 2 pages then it has irrelevant information to the role. Cut back and make it **R**elevant!

B. Readable

There are so many ways to make your resume readable and presentable. Yet, many candidates do not make it easy for the employer to read their resumes. Some examples of confusing practices include:

- inconsistent font sizes
- large headers / footers
- multiple section subheadings
- narrow page margins
- not clearly divided sections
- overflow of colours
- overuse of acronyms
- small line spacings
- too much **Bold** / *Italic* text.

Your resume might be the best and the most relevant to the job, but if the employer or the Applicant Tracking System (ATS) cannot easily recognise key information, then it will most likely be dismissed. You want to make it as easy as possible for the employer and the ATS to obtain key information, so make it **R**eadable.

C. Reviewed

Review your resume. The elementary act of reading with a fresh pair of eyes or having someone else to read over it can surprise you with the number of mistakes you will find. Even if you spent days on it, do NOT submit a resume without thoroughly reviewing it.

There are many things to look for in your review. These include:

- **Consistency:** Be consistent. As an example, if you have your responsibilities described in a paragraph format for one role, do the same for all roles. Similarly, if you mentioned two key achievements in one role, it only makes sense to do the same for the other ones.

- **Grammar:** Read and reread the phrases and sentences in your resume, and check for any grammatical errors. In case of doubt, always opt to simplify, not complicate the language used.

- **Language:** Your resume is an official document, and the language there should be formal, so no slang or casual language to be used. Also, do not use abbreviations or terms that are only known to your company and not in the wider industry.

- **Lists:** If you have chosen a particular style of dot points when listing information (triangles, small dots, squares...etc.), ensure the same list style is followed across all roles and sections.

- **Spelling:** Double check that the spell check is activated so the spelling is consistent with the country of application. In this case, it is Australian English as opposed to US English, so you are organised, not organized!

Ensure your resume is Reviewed, so you are confident that it has passed all *The Three 'R's* making it Relevant, Readable and Reviewed.

3.5 Cover Letters

When it comes to cover letters, they do have a mixed perception in the industry. Some hiring managers insist on reading them word by word, while others do not pay much attention to them. Nonetheless, as a graduate, why would you take your chances? Include a good cover letter for all of your applications, if there is an option to do so.

Writing a strong persuasive cover letter can prove to be advantageous in such a competitive job market. Your resume will always be the main selling tool, but a cover letter acts as a powerful supporting document.

You want to sell yourself here, highlighting any relevant achievements to the company. The more direct you are in the cover letter, the more appealing it will be.

The three main elements to a cover letter are:

1. **You**: Who you are as a professional, and what you possess in terms of experience, achievements and transferable skills.

2. **The company**: What you know about the company (values, culture...etc.) and what has attracted you to work there.

3. **The role**: What makes you a good fit for the role, and what value do you bring to it.

Cover these three points in no more than one page while addressing the person in charge (by name if known), and then reference your resume, before thanking the employer for their time and consideration.

I will not go into further detail here, since cover letters vary greatly depending on the role and context. But if you address the three main elements in a concise and a professional manner, then (along with the resume) you have a compelling application.

3.6 LinkedIn

LinkedIn is not exactly the first platform you'll think about during your studies. As a matter of fact, A 2019 US social media study conducted by Edison Research found that students compromised only 5% of total LinkedIn users there! That's not surprising, as many students refer to LinkedIn as a "professional Facebook".

Personally, after being active for some time on the LinkedIn platform, I believe that LinkedIn is a lot more than a professional Facebook. To put it simply: If you are not on LinkedIn, you are not serious about your job search! You don't think so? Let's talk numbers.

As of late 2020, there are over 700 million LinkedIn users globally, 11 million of which are in Australia. 40% of all LinkedIn users are active on a daily basis. Further, around 55 job applications are submitted every second, with 7 seconds being the time between every hire on LinkedIn. The overwhelming majority of recruiters (87%) find LinkedIn the most effective tool when vetting candidates during the hiring process.

I can go on with similar statistics, but I think you get the idea. If you missed signing up to LinkedIn earlier in your degree, waste no time!

Assuming you don't have a profile on LinkedIn, let's get started on what needs to be done.

1. *Sign up with your full name*

   Your full name is your first and last names. If you had a previous name, or have a preferred nickname, you can always add it in brackets. Use your real name as this makes it easier for previous contacts to recognise you when you add them, or find you from their end when searching your name.

2. Add a professional shot

If you don't have one, please don't add a cropped photo of one your nights out! It's better in this case to leave your profile without a photo. This is your professional brand so you should invest time (and money if you must) to enhance it. Some university Career Centres have a studio that you can use. If not, there are many freelancers who specialise in exactly that. Word of mouth and Google are your best friends.

If you absolutely can't find anyone, ask a friend to take a shot with an iPhone in portrait mode, with a plain or not-so-distracting background. LinkedIn profiles with photos get 21x more views and 36x more messages. You have no excuse for not having a profile photo at this point.

3. Add a cover photo

The very fact that you changed your standard grey cover photo (used to be blue) gives you more credibility and removes you from having a 'default' profile, which almost every newbie on LinkedIn has. Boardrooms, offices, nature, city landscapes, or something related to your industry are all great options. There are thousands of free-to-use stock photos online. Get creative!

4. Add a headline

The headline will appear just below your professional photo. This item should be short, catchy, and describe what makes you unique. It can also be your current job title (if you have one). You want to make your headline stand out by describing your primary skill or ability.

For example, "*Aspiring Leader | Enthusiastic Accountant | Seeking Internships In The Banking Industry*" sounds better than "*Accounting student at X university looking for a job*". You might not believe it, but there are hundreds of students who have "*looking for a job*" as their headline.

Ensure that all words in your headline start with an uppercase letter (so it's '*Seeking*' not '*seeking*'), and that you highlight your qualities to the employer instead of just asking for a job. Your headline is essentially the online brand that you're putting out there to the world.

Your headline, name and photo are the first things a LinkedIn user sees when searching LinkedIn and discovering your profile. Those elements determine whether or not the reader will click through to your full profile, so invest the time to ace them.

5. *Add your education & work experience*

This should be self-explanatory on LinkedIn. You want to add your volunteering experience, your work experience (be it internships or casual jobs) and any additional involvement you had through your degree. A recent LinkedIn survey found that over 40% of professionals stated that when they are evaluating candidates, they consider volunteer work equally as valuable as paid work experience.

When you are describing your responsibilities, focus on transferable skills. For example, instead of just saying, *"Served customers"*, you can say, *"Oversaw the service of over 150 customers daily, while successfully managing customer complaints and resolving them promptly."* There are many ways to describe the same responsibility in an impactful way, so do your best to optimise this section.

6. *Add a summary*

Also known as the 'About' section. This section tells the employer what you are all about. Again, *"looking for a job"* is not a good summary. Draw on your skills and what you offer to the organisation first, and then specify what type of opportunities you are currently seeking.

For the summary, you do not need to tell your life story over two pages, a paragraph or two will do. See the paragraph below as a template with some *suggestions*, and tailor yours according to your needs. You can add a second paragraph to make this section more personal. There are no right or wrong ways to talk about yourself. Ensure that your summary is telling the reader what you have to offer, and where you want to take your career.

"I am a *dynamic and people-focused / result-driven / detail-oriented* professional, possessing over X years experience in the *Construction Management / Consulting / Financial Services* Industry, with particular hands-on experience in delivering wide range of projects. A trusted *Professional / Analyst / Accountant / Engineer / Consultant* with proven expertise in *Customer Service / Project Management /*

Leadership Initiatives / Business Development / Community Engagement. Seeking the next *challenge / opportunity / role* in the *Financial Services / Management Consulting / Digital Marketing / Construction* industry."

7. *Add the relevant skills*

According to LinkedIn, listing five or more skills on your LinkedIn profile can lead to up to 17 times more views! What skills should you add? Start with the direct ones that you have acquired through your degree, which are in demand almost anywhere: Communication, Teamwork, Presentation, Microsoft Office and Problem-Solving.

After that, get more specific about the skills you have. For example, Microsoft Excel and Microsoft PowerPoint can be added separately. Similarly, Leadership and Management can be added as different skills (because they are).

I encourage you to look in the job ads for key skills and add them to your profile (if you have them, of course). For example, a programming role might need SQL, C++, Java and Python as skills, or just some of them. Add the ones you are comfortable with and are relevant to your targeted roles.

To conclude this section, it's better to list more skills that you are comfortable with, than to miss on a role because you forgot to mention a required skill. You can always explain yourself and your level of competence against the role requirements in the interview, but not adding some skills could mean no interview at all!

3.7 Network, Network, Network!

Well, here comes my networking plug! I cannot emphasise this enough. Networking is crucial for you at this stage, as you're actively seeking a graduate role.

While we are still in the LinkedIn mood, it is worth noting that 78% of respondents to a 2020 LinkedIn survey cited a strong network as a key way to get ahead. How does one network on LinkedIn? Here are three quick tips:

1. Add everyone from your other social networks to your LinkedIn (No, not that random person you met at a hostel six years ago). I mean friends, colleagues and family members you have on Instagram, Facebook, WhatsApp...etc. You can easily get 100+ connections from this exercise! Furthermore, if you still have access to your student email or you use a second email, import that to LinkedIn. You may be surprised with some of the suggested connections. Remember, this is not Facebook, so connecting with someone does not mean they have to be a close friend. Just connect!

2. If you met someone recently at a job fair, or another professional event, connect with them using a simple message on LinkedIn (see examples on the next page). Trust me, it goes a long way, you never know how beneficial a connection might be in a few years.

3. Let's say you connected with everyone you know, and you are still not up to the magic 500+ connections on LinkedIn. You can connect with people you have not met in person on LinkedIn! No, I am not suggesting you connect with randoms. Connect with professionals

you have things in common with: Same industry, same university, same employer (former or current), similar interests and LinkedIn groups, or have several mutual connections.

On the last point of connecting with someone you have not met, NEVER ask for a job in your first message. This is not the way to establish quality connections, not only because it seldom works, but also because it might lead to resentment from the other side.

Personally, I accept every connection request I get (with the exception of Bitcoin traders, you know the ones I am talking about). Further, I accept connection requests without an attached note, but the reality is that not everyone on LinkedIn does. Adding a simple note goes a long way in establishing that quality connection (as discussed in Chapter 2).

What to say instead of asking for a job? Ask for insights or experience. People do not like to feel that they're being taken advantage of (in the case of a job ask), but would love to help and offer their insights when they know that their advice is appreciated. Once you read the person's profile and get to know what they do, your connection request messages can read something like these:

> *"Hi John, great profile you have here, would love to connect and know more about you."*

> *"Hi John, I see you're also part of the Swinburne alumni network, would be great to connect."*

> *"Hi John, Looks like you also worked at ANZ, let's connect."*

"Hi John, I see you help graduates with jobs, any tips for me? I am graduating from my Business degree in July."

"Hi John, hope you're well. Since we both work in Financial Services, would love to connect."

"Hi John, great meeting you at X event, would love to stay in touch."

As you see, you did not have to send a long message or ask for a job. And yes, I did use "Hi" and not "Dear", as it's a short message not an email, and the context is already there.

Personally, I have received similar messages in the past and responded to all of them. I know for a fact the majority of professionals on LinkedIn would do so (at least based on my experience).

Let's say for some reason the recipient does not respond or accept your connection request. So what? That is one less connection you never had! Remember that you miss 100% of the shots you don't take!

I will conclude this section by mentioning the fact that I have never met (in person) one of the five professionals interviewed in Chapter 4! Our relationship has been based entirely on our interactions on LinkedIn (and of course that Zoom Interview). So, take every opportunity as a graduate to network, and know as many people as you possibly can. Remember, your network is your net-worth.

3.8 Interview Preparation

Congrats! You have done it all. You've found the role, you've written a great resume and cover letter, you've applied for the job (or were referred by someone). Now it's the final step to get that job: The interview. This is your time to shine.

You may or may not have done a professional interview before. In my case, I've only interviewed for casual roles in hospitality, as I've never been interviewed for an office job until my final year.

Interviews do take many formats, such as in-person, virtual, group interviews with assessment centres, panel interviews... etc. One thing you MUST ask about beforehand is the type of interview you will be having, and who will be there. Then, you should search the interviewer online (by a Google search or on LinkedIn).

While it is impossible to cover every single interview question here, let's address some common interview questions in detail. We will focus on both general and behaviour-based questions.

3.8.1. General Questions

1. *Tell me about yourself*

   You will almost certainly be asked the famous '*Tell me about yourself*' question. For this question, the interviewer is not interested in your childhood hobbies, but rather in what you studied, the type of skills you can bring to the table, as well as what you are seeking in the next role. Always remember to keep your answer short and straight to the point. Don't make your answer too brief, but it shouldn't be ten minutes either. Aim for a minute or two, highlighting your education, relevant experience and skills for the role.

2. *What do you know about us?*

   Again, you will most certainly be asked about what you know in regards to the company. If you answer something along the lines of, '*I know it is a really big company with a lot of opportunities there and would love to be part of it*', sorry to tell you, but that is not the right answer. Your answer should demonstrate that you have done extensive research about the company. As such, you should know about the company values, where the company operates geographically, what divisions they have, what type of growth they are experiencing, and what you understand the role to be. The more detailed you are here, the better your answer will be, as it demonstrates that you've done your research as opposed to someone who just wants a job.

   The information you are seeking about the company should be public, so do spend some time doing your homework before the interview. If you are struggling to find all the information, then try to ask someone who works there or is in the same sector.

3. *Why do you think that you are the right candidate?*

Another common interview question is, *'What makes you think that you are the right candidate?'* Some variation of this question would be *'Why should we hire you?'* or *'What makes you a good fit for the role?'* The wrong answer would be *'Because I am great'* or *'Because I believe I have the skills you need'*. Such short and self-centred responses would not sit well with the interviewer. A good answer could be *'As someone who worked in such and such (name the industry), I believe I possess vital skills for the role such as (list relevant skills), in addition to my involvement in (campus activity / academic achievement). I understand you are seeking a candidate who is (name candidate qualities), and I believe I bring a lot of value and relevant skills, which make me a great fit for the role'*.

Always remember to frame your answer around the value and the addition you bring to the role, as opposed to just mentioning your own personal qualities.

4. *What is your biggest weakness?*

If you respond with, *'I don't have any'*, that is a definite failure for this question. A good response would be one that demonstrates your weakness, but then talks about what you are doing to improve it.

For example, you could say, *'In some previous projects, I have always struggled with delegation. Although I understand that some tasks cannot be handed to someone else, I often find myself more than I should on my own, without giving other members a chance. To address that, I have been proactive in my communication to other team members, with clear task delegations at the earlier stages of the project. I believe I became better at it and was able to focus more on coordination, and ensuring that I'm available to support where needed, as opposed to unnecessarily doing everything on my own'.*

There are tens of other examples that you can mention here. The key is to always mention the weakness, and then speak to what you've done to address it.

Also, make sure that the weakness does not directly relate to the role you are applying for. For example, if you are an IT graduate, definitely do not mention your weakness as dealing with computers or new technologies. You might be surprised, but this has happened, and naturally resulted in elimination from the recruitment process.

3.8.2. Behaviour-Based Questions

Regardless of the interview format, you are likely to be asked some behaviour-based questions. A common way to address such questions is the **STAR** format: **S**ituation, **T**ask, **A**ction and **R**esult. Let's discuss it by providing some sample questions.

'Tell us about a time where you had to go above and beyond to deliver a project on time?'

'Tell us about a time where you had a conflict with your colleague?'

'Tell us about a time where you failed to meet a deadline?'

'Tell us about a time where things did not go as planned, what did you do and what was the result?'

All of the previous questions can be addressed with a couple of experiences from your degree or a previous role. Have your STAR responses ready before the interview. Do not improvise on the day. Let's answer a couple of them as examples:

1. *Tell us about a time where you had to go above and beyond to deliver a project on time?*

   'Back in my final year project, we were assessed as a group. Initially, we agreed that each member had to finalise their allocated presentation slides so we could present as a group. Given that the slides of one group member were not up to standard in terms of format, I had to go over the final slides at the last minute, compiling them again in the new format. I had to then update all members accordingly before our presentation, so we could get the extra formatting

marks. I made sure that we caught up and rehearsed the full presentation twice on the day before the class. As a result, we got the highest mark in the class, and were named the best group presenters for that unit.'

As you can see, the answer outlined the **Situation,** which is the group presentation not being complete, the **Task,** which is having to complete the presentation slides before the day, the **Action,** which is you having to do it yourself and update all members, and the **Result,** which is achieving the highest mark in the class.

2. *Tell us about a time where you failed to meet a deadline?*

'In my first year of studies, I underestimated the research involved for one of my business subjects, which in turn led me to submit the assignment after the due date. As a result, I barely passed the subject with a conceded pass. From that moment on, I decided to finish all of my assignments and submit them at least one day before the deadline. I am proud to say that I have not failed to meet a deadline since, as evident in my academic achievements.'

Again, similar to the previous response, it followed the **STAR** format. For this example, the **Situation** is that you missed the assignment's deadline and almost failed. The **Task** is that you have to ensure that this never happens again. The **Action** is that you now finish everything in advance and submit it one day before the deadline. Finally, the **Result** is that you have not missed a deadline since, and achieved high grades.

As discussed earlier, these are only a few examples that address behaviour-based questions. The key takeaway is that you do not want to make up things or improvise on the day. Prepare your **STAR** responses and rehearse them before the interview.

Now that you are familiar with some of the most common interview questions, it is worth noting that the interviewer does not know what your prepared answer was. So, if you deviate during your response, do not overthink it or try to drastically change your response, just keep the flow going. You will sound more confident answering flawlessly, than if you paused multiple times during your response.

Remember that the person interviewing you is a human being. Act naturally and be yourself.

Finally, as I cannot possibly cover all the interview scenarios, I am providing you with some insights on what to focus on and what to avoid doing in interviews, based on some common graduates' interview behaviour. Here are some DOs and DON'Ts for your interview.

3.8.3 Interview DOs & DON'Ts

#	DO	DON'T
1	Overdress or dress formally if you're not sure how you should dress. Look your best.	Underestimate your personal presentation and hygiene.
2	Arrive at least 10 minutes before the interview time (Yes, 10 or even 15 minutes if you can).	Be late! It is almost impossible to land a position if you are late, so don't be.
3	Switch off your phone or put it in airplane mode before entry.	Look at your phone or watch during the interview, as it does not send the right message.
4	Smile and offer a firm handshake when you meet the interviewer.	Speak with a soft voice when introducing yourself; be confident and project yourself.
5	Pay attention to the name of the person / people interviewing you, and engage with everyone in the room.	Make eye contact with only one person in a panel interview.
6	Use polite and formal language if unsure.	Use slang words unless reciprocating the interviewer's language.
7	Ask questions at the end. (Could be about the person, the role or the training for example).	Say that you have no questions to ask at the end.
8	Ask about the next steps or when you should hear back from them.	Bring up the salary conversation unless you were asked to.

#	DO	DON'T
9	Provide a range to your remuneration when asked. (If you have to, put a number based on your research).	Go to the interview without researching in detail the salary ranges for the role.
10	Send a thank you note to the person who interviewed you.	Contact them before the time they said they would get back to you.

In this chapter, you may have noticed that we didn't discuss degree specifics like majors, subjects or grades, but rather covered a wide range of cross-industry practices and job search techniques. This is exactly the point. You have already been told throughout your degree about doing well in your studies to find a job. But as you know by now, there is a bit more to it.

To conclude, given the actionable advice provided in this chapter, I encourage you to reread it when needed. The information provided acts as a reference to guide your graduate job search. As such, tailor the learnings here to your own journey, and **TARGET** your dream job!

GROW   ACQUIRE   TARGET   **EMBRACE**

CHAPTER 4
EMBRACE
(GRADUATE)

This is it. You have now graduated, understood what you are supposed to do, and started your graduate journey. You are (in theory) in a position to find your dream role. You may have already found one. But the reality is, you may still question your graduate journey, regardless whether you've found a job or not by now.

As a matter of fact, you may still have no clue what jobs you want to apply for, or what your passion is. That's ok, that was me too. Upskilling, doing further studies, starting a business, or studying another degree are all viable options, and so are changing jobs and careers after your first job.

Every graduate journey is different, and my graduate journey may resemble some or none of yours. But don't just take my word for it. I have interviewed five professionals who are either industry leaders or young professionals, and asked them to share their own insights about the graduate journey.

The professionals interviewed here are from different educational and career backgrounds. Some were passionate about their field of choice, while others figured it out on the way. Nevertheless, there is one clear thing they all agree on, and that is: **Network, Network, Network!**

I ask you to pay attention to their stories and advice so you can learn and unlearn what the graduate journey is all about, which translates to you embracing your own journey.[*]

---

* While I aim to provide diverse opinions on the matter, two of the female professionals lined up could not make the interview after initial acceptance, due to personal events at the time of the interview.

4.1 Professional Graduate Insights

4.1.1. Amit Naik
Management Consultant Manager, Accenture

i) Thank you for taking the time to join us today. Tell us about yourself in terms of your background, namely educational and professional backgrounds.

My name is Amit. I was born and raised in Zimbabwe, Africa.

In 2011, I moved to Australia for my tertiary education. My undergraduate degree was a Bachelor of Information Technology and Systems at Monash University in Melbourne followed by a Master of Management degree at the University of Melbourne.

After finishing my Master's in 2015, I successfully secured my permanent residency and relocated to Sydney for a job at Ernst and Young (EY). At EY, I was a Consultant in the Tech Advisory team providing strategy and consulting services across several industries such as government education and retail and consumer goods. Within two years I was promoted to a Senior Consultant.

Then in 2018, I managed to secure a consulting opportunity in Melbourne at Accenture, where I am today. Currently, I am in the Strategy & Consulting team within management consulting. I have been working on large and multinational utility and mining organisations. My role involves analysing organisation process and system, designing future state business processes and managing the deployment of large-scale implementations.

ii) So, back to your university days. What was Amit like as a grad? Did you always know what you wanted to do?

As a grad I was all about networking to develop genuine relationships and connections to ensure more opportunities to advance my career.

I have always had a business mindset, but it was at a later stage during tertiary studies when I decided that I wanted to work in Consulting. During my Masters, I did a Consulting Course called the Global Business Practicum. It took me to Shanghai to provide consulting services to a company, and it was during this experience that I realised consulting was what I wanted to do.

I found it interesting and challenging being in a client environment where you need to understand the client's needs, challenges and aspirations. You're given a problem that you need to analyse to provide solutions through understanding the industry and the organisation.

So, when I graduated from my Masters, it was through my network and their experiences that I was able to figure out the best way forward for me. I heard about consulting in the Big-4 and decided to apply and got priceless guidance from experienced friends on how to be successful during the process.

iii) Knowing what you know now, what did you do that worked and would you have done differently or expect other graduates to have done?

What worked for me is perseverance. Going back to my application with EY, I was aware that I was not a permanent resident at the time and that would make my chances tougher. I called the HR department and asked them to consider me regardless as I was aware that my Permanent Residence (PR) grant was on the horizon. They took it on board, I got an interview and they gave me a job offer! I do not expect anyone reading this to start calling companies, but what I am trying to say is challenge the status quo, understand where your weaknesses are against other candidates and work on trying to turn those weaknesses into strengths.

I would ask myself back then, *'What's the worst thing that could happen?'* I knew that if I just tried at anything, the worst-case scenario would be getting rejected or declined, and I had to make myself understand that I should be fine with that. What was most important was that I did not go forward looking backwards, or in other words, that I didn't have any regrets.

In regards to what I would have done differently, I would have started networking at an earlier stage in my tertiary education and got more involved in campus and extracurricular activities during my undergrad years. I would have searched LinkedIn and established connections with recruiters to understand what they are looking for and their insights into roles and organisations. I would have also searched for mentors who had career paths that seemed of interest to me and reached out to them for guidance and advice.

Remember as a graduate, you are not expected to be an expert in your field of choice. Eagerness to learn, curiosity and sheer motivation and drive are good qualities of a graduate. Be a good communicator show a level of problem solving and adaptability. The rest can be learned on the job.

iv) That's a wide range of skills you mentioned there. Can you tell us a bit more about your campus involvement?

Naturally, I think I am an introverted person, however as you may recall I emphasised the importance of building your network. This is achievable in a variety of social, academic and professional ways. At university, I played in a Hockey team, joined various clubs and societies, and also became a residential advisor on campus. Such involvement played a vital role in strengthening soft skills for being more employable.

So, get involved and network as much as you can! The more networking you do, the more opportunities you'll have.

v) You mentioned earlier that you relocated from Melbourne to Sydney and back, what would you advise graduates who are hesitant to relocate?

I am a strong believer that travel and understanding different cultures and ways of life is one of the best educations you can receive.

Everyone is different in regard to their preferences and everyone is in different stages of their lives, which in turn will factor into a decision to relocate or not. For me personally, being an international student at the time and not having strong ties to either city, I was happy to follow where the opportunity took me on both occasions.

What I would advise those who are considering relocation is to not be shy about asking your employers for a relocation allowance to help cover costs. Ask if there is anyone in the organisation that you can "buddy up" with that can provide insights on different areas to live in, cost of living and transportation requirements. If you are open to travel, do not restrict yourself to one state, opportunities open up once work experience is established.

vi) What are your biggest learnings from the change that COVID-19 brought to our lives in 2020?

I believe ways of working has had to be completely reimagined in 2020. From a consulting point of view, adapting to working remotely was easy as consultants have autonomous workstyle.

However, consultants are augmented into client workforces, so fostering relationships and developing deep knowledge of client organisations became a bit of a challenge. Virtual coffee catch-ups became the new norm which was an unnatural, but necessary to remain personable.

I believe flexible work arrangements will be part of the future once normality is restored. Whilst being able to work from home has its pros and cons, work-life balance discipline will need to be reinstated due to longer working hours.

vii) Any parting thoughts for the 2021 graduates and beyond?

Be hungry, be curious, and just keep trying! Transitioning from studying to working can often be scary due to the uncertainty of what the road ahead holds. There's always a feeling of uncertainty of "what's next?" Once you make the transition to the next level, you'll realise that all will be fine. There's nothing to fear. The same applies to the work environment. You'll be fine. Embrace the uncertainty and be confident!

In the words of the rolling stones – *'You can't always get what you want, but if you try sometimes, well, you might find you get what you need.'*

viii) Thanks for your time and insights, Amit. It's much appreciated. Finally, what's the best way to contact you?

The best way to contact me would be through my LinkedIn: **Amit Naik**.

4.1.2. Dom Jennings
Managing Consultant, Robert Walters

i) Thank you for taking the time to join us today. Tell us about yourself in terms of your background, namely educational and professional backgrounds.

Thanks for having me!

So, about myself – I'm a Kiwi, born and raised in a small country town about an hour outside of Auckland in New Zealand. As a child, I attended a small local primary school, and then attended a boarding school in Auckland called Sacred Heart College.

After completing college, I studied at Auckland University of Technology, completing a Bachelor of Business with a major in Marketing and International Business.

After university, I started working for an Events company in Auckland, doing a combination role with a bit of marketing, a bit of event management and a bit of business development.

In 2018, I made the move to Melbourne and joined Robert Walters, one of the world's biggest recruitment agencies. Today, I'm a Managing Consultant with Robert Walters' Projects and Transformation team, specialising in recruiting Project and Program Managers for companies all across the city.

ii) So, as recruiters typically have a Human Resources background, tell us about your career transition upon relocation.

When I decided to move to Melbourne, I realised that I wanted a change from what I had been doing. I was burnt out and needed a new challenge. When I was trying to work out what I wanted my next challenge to be, I decided to look at what skills I was bringing to the table.

I realised that I was good at building relationships and communicating with people. I'd also done a lot of business development in my previous role, so thought a sales-focused role would be a good fit.

Coincidently, as I was looking at options, I was contacted through LinkedIn by a Robert Walters' internal recruiter, asking if I had considered recruitment as a career.

I thought about it and, although it wasn't necessarily something I had looked at previously, I realised it aligned with my skills of sales and business development, and also was an opportunity to really help people, which is something that really resonated with me.

After thinking about it for a while, I decided it was the job for me so I made the jump, and I haven't looked back!

iii) On your relocation from Auckland to Melbourne, what would you advise graduates who are hesitant to relocate?

I was fortunate, in that I was able to secure my role while I was still in NZ thanks to virtual interviews (and in a post-COVID world, that's even more acceptable!) but for those who don't have the same luxury, just do your research before you leave.

Speak to a recruiter in the area you want to work in, speak to people in the industry, and see if you have any friends who live there. Wherever you can, familiarising yourself with what to expect when you arrive will make that eventual transition easier.

iv) As a recruiter, what does a typical workday look like for you?

In my role, I'm what's known as a 360-degree consultant. That means I look after the two sides of recruitment: the client side which deals with managers who are looking to bring someone into their team, and then I work with jobseekers looking for jobs too.

Typically, I'm out and about for a lot of the day, meeting with candidates and clients. It's not uncommon (again, pre-COVID) for me to be having 4-5 coffee meetings in a day which can be a lot of caffeine!

v) What was Dom like as a grad? Did you always know what you wanted to do?

I had absolutely no idea what I wanted to do!

Coming out of high school, I actually thought I wanted to be a lawyer! Honestly, with the benefit of hindsight, I'm really thankful that I didn't go down that path – I don't think I would have gotten past the first year of law school!

Instead, I ended up doing a Bachelor of Business with a major in Marketing and International Business. I believe that my university degree gave me quite a lot of flexibility and a fairly broad view of the different sectors within the industry. Marketing gave me some specialisation while Business provided a wider view.

After completing my degree, I found myself not knowing what I wanted to do again. However, while I was in my final year, a family friend who was running an event management company approached me to see if I wanted to help out with some part-time work while studying. I didn't mind a bit of extra money coming in, so I took it.

Working in that role, I quickly realised that I really enjoyed it, especially the opportunity to travel and meet people, so much so I ended up working in the events industry for five years!

To the graduates reading this, this is my experience. Yours may be completely different. Unlike me, you may be certain about your passion upon graduating. If that's the case, pursue it. But it's also important to know that not everyone has such certainty. That said, your path might change even if you have a great level of certainty regarding what you want. But what's important is to acquire enough skills so you can be flexible and follow whichever path you choose to take.

Further to that, your passion doesn't necessarily have to be your job. You don't have to marry the two immediately. For example, you're really passionate about marketing so you must do everything possible to secure a marketing degree and a job in that field later on.

I think it's more of what you're passionate about in life, generally. I believe when you're passionate about something; it makes things a lot easier. If you're passionate enough about something and you're involved in that area, you'll find a job within its field or one that utilises your skills.

vi) Given your role, let's talk about resumes / CVs and cover letters. What are the common mistakes you find people tend to commit? And what are your tips to create good ones?

On one hand, some people think that cover letters are redundant and that you don't need them. On the other hand, others think that they're essential. I would say that you're never going to be rejected from a job application by including a cover letter, so it's worth including one!

I believe cover letters should be geared towards the organisation that you're applying to rather than about yourself. Think about their requirements. What do they need? How can you fill that need? How can you be valuable to them?

Your cover letter should be about answering any of their questions and making it clear to them that you're ticking every box they need or, if not, how you'll be able to grow and develop into the person they need.

As for the biggest mistake I see in CVs, it's all about the attention to detail. It's not anything major but it definitely matters. Using the correct spelling and grammar is essential because you're really trying to put your best foot forward. You don't want to give the recruiter a reason to turn you down for a role. So, make sure you use the correct spelling and have really good grammar in your CV. You can use tools like the spell check function in Microsoft Word to help you with these.

As for the work experience part, one of the biggest pieces of advice that I give job seekers is to separate your achievements from your responsibilities in your previous roles. Employers are quite keen to know what your achievements are. They want to see where you were able to add value to the organisations you've worked for. For example, you were able to reduce the number of errors in a certain report by X% or you were able to increase revenue by $X.

Obviously, it's a little bit different if you're a graduate who's looking for your first role. In that case, I'd recommend listing the responsibilities you might have had while working part-time and studying. Other than that, think of what transferable skills you have and mention those.

Personally, one of the things I try to gauge when reading a CV is a person's written communication skills. I think it's one of the top skills or the most in demand. In particular, I'm talking about the ability to communicate concisely, which is a critical skill for professionals looking to move up in their career field.

One way of showing that you have good written communication skills is to make sure that your CV is easy to read. You don't want huge blocks of text. Just keep it to bullet points. It's a great and effective technique when mentioning your work experiences.

Given that, make sure that what you're talking about in your CV is actually related to the job. This means your CV should be an extension of your cover letter, which explains why you're good for the role.

Finally, I'd like to share a quote which I recently encountered. *'Attitude determines altitude.'* This means that if you've got the right attitude to work, that you're willing to put as much effort as you can and you're willing to learn and grow, that makes you incredibly attractive as an employee, even if you don't tick all of the boxes in a specific job description.

vii) This brings us to our next question about interviews. They can be intimidating, even for experienced professionals. Knowing that most graduates have never done a professional interview before, what would you advise them?

I agree. Having your first interview can be nerve wracking and daunting. But two of the things I value are actually honesty and vulnerability. If a candidate came in and said, *'Look. This is the first interview I've done in a long time...'*, I would instantly kind of let my guard down. Ultimately, people are— most of the time— understanding when it comes to these things.

Another scenario is if you say something like *'Look. I may not be as good as other people that you've got in terms of experience but this is what I bring to the table: I'm a really hard worker. I'm really dedicated. I'm going to do everything I can to prove myself.'* These are the statements that an interviewer will really pick up on. These are what show to your potential employer, what we call soft skills.

To be clear, there are two sides when it comes to skills. First, there are the required technical skills, which are directly related to the role such as proficiency in using certain software. Then second, you have the soft skills.

Over the past 20 years, it's clear that soft skills are becoming more and more important for employers. Actually, we have clients telling us that a candidate's soft side, cultural fit and aptitude to learn is more important than their technical skills. This is because technical skills can be taught. But it's very hard to teach someone work ethics or instil in them the willingness to learn. In short, being honest and vulnerable along with demonstrating your value to the employer is critical in an interview.

One more thing I'd like to add is that no one is going to absolutely nail the very first interview. But given the fact that someone asked you to come in for one, it means they saw something in your CV, which told them that you may be a good fit for the role. Given that, it's absolutely critical for you to practise. It's important to have self-confidence. When you practise, speak loud and clear. It doesn't matter whether you rehearse with someone in person or via a video call or even if you're just facing a mirror.

Other than that, do your research on the organisation if you haven't done so. Find out what they do, what their principles and values are and what kind of culture they have. Knowing these gives you an insight into what they need from the employee they want to hire.

For example, an organisation looking for an entry-level customer service assistant will ask you about how you deal with people. They'd want to know how you handle situations with difficult people. So, think about what relevant experiences you have which would tell them that you have what they're looking for..

viii) What are your views on the importance of LinkedIn?

LinkedIn is the platform of the future. I think it's important for any job seeker to have a presence on LinkedIn. Even if you think it might be less important in your first couple of years at university, you'll see its importance once you start looking for professional work.

A few years ago, LinkedIn was mainly used to connect with people that you knew. Now, it's becoming a lot more of a social network which allows you to expand your professional network.

By being active on LinkedIn and engaging with people like putting your opinion on a viral post, it can be a really good way to build a public profile or image which often leads to opportunities. I, like many, have been approached about opportunities on LinkedIn.

Besides LinkedIn, another platform I'd like to mention is Seek. It's, in my opinion, the most powerful platform for job seekers in Australia.

ix) What are your biggest learnings from the change that COVID-19 brought to our lives in 2020?

A lot has changed this year. What I've personally learned is that people are resilient. They can adapt pretty quickly when they have to.

Our organisation, for example, established a pretty good set-up in terms of mobility and the ability to work remotely. When it comes to the wider job market and the workforce in general, things that previously would've been an absolute last resort like electronic or video interviews are now essential!

Given that, being adaptable is a very important skill for workers. For graduates, this relates to realising what's out of your control and making the best of what you've got.

x) Thanks for your time and insights, Dom. It's much appreciated. Finally, what's the best way to contact you?

My email address is probably the best way to reach me. It's **Dominic.Jennings@RobertWalters.com.au**. You can also reach me via LinkedIn: **Dom Jennings**.

4.1.3. Jamal Elamsy
Global Sales Manager, Platinum Health

i) Thank you for taking the time to join us today. Tell us about yourself in terms of your background, namely educational and professional backgrounds.

My name is Jamal. I'm Palestinian. I lived in the Middle East for the majority of my life. When I turned 18, I moved to Australia to pursue my engineering degree.

As you know, being from an Arab background, people think you're a failure if you're not a lawyer, engineer or doctor! I was no different so I chose to take up telecommunications engineering.

Outside my studies and on a personal level, I'd say I'm more of a disciplined, driven and a very motivated person. I want to be one of the top businessmen in the world. And I'm working towards that with my ventures at the moment. I do exporting and importing as a business in the medical supplies shipping industry.

ii) So, what was Jamal like as a grad? Did you always know what you wanted to do?

Let me take you back to the time before my university days, if I may.

Actually, I didn't want to go to university. I wanted to be a professional soccer player. But my dad rejected the idea so it didn't happen. Still, I took that passion and used it to become a high achiever. From then on, I've aimed to do the best I can in my life, from my studies to my relationships. I tell myself,

'You've got to put your 100% in it.' I'm a '100% or nothing' type of person, either I go all in or not.

In saying that, I chose a double degree in engineering and business. But I dropped the latter because I realised that business courses are really basic. You can read and teach yourself everything through Google or YouTube.

Now, about my engineering degree, I believe I really did well not just on its technical aspect, but also when it comes to paying attention in general. I paid attention during lectures. In particular, I observed the students who were focused on the lectures. They were the ones committed to getting high distinctions (HDs) and were top performers.

Slowly, I started to get myself involved with them. And this led to creating a network of smart people with different skills. Back then, I believed that even if I didn't know everything about a given subject, I could always collaborate within my network. And then together, we could achieve our goals.

For example, in our software development course, I had no idea what C++ was along with other programming languages. After I failed the initial assessment, I did whatever it took to get the HD overall for the unit. Due to that, I set my standard to always be number one.

By consistently putting in the effort required to reach and maintain that, I got High Distinctions in all of my 24 units.

iii) What a standard to have! So, on that, tell us about your graduate employment journey.

Well, if we go back to my university days, I didn't work for the first two years. My dad had the impression that I should only focus on my studies and getting good grades. After protesting for months, and the fact that I wanted financial independence, I convinced him that it's okay for me to work on a casual or part-time basis.

What I didn't know was that it was really difficult to get a job in retail, because I didn't have any previous experience. So in my resume, I spoke more about a fitness role I did for a short time back home. In particular, I focused on its customer service aspect.

My first retail employer considered it as experience. After working for some time, I realised I didn't exactly like my retail role. But that's the whole point of university life: to try as many things as possible.

From retail, I went to work in telemarketing and door-to-door sales. I learnt a lot about presentation and customer service skills through those jobs.

Then at some point, I wanted to find an internship.

I submitted several applications and got rejected by more than 200 companies. I still have all those rejection emails from big companies like IBM, Cisco, and Telstra to the small ones—all the companies that didn't want any part of me.

At the end of the day, I used the international network that I had. Through it, I got an internship in Dubai, which I did for six months. I went back to Australia after that and continued my degree. During that time, I worked in sales again in a marketing agency. Even though I was working almost for free back then, I gained a lot of skills during my four-months stint there. I acquired important skills that made me more employable later on.

Now, I'm aware that most graduates want to get paid for their work. It shows that you're not undervaluing yourself, which is how it should be. But if you're not getting any job offers, try to do free work. Then, once you get the skills, you'll go places and people will want you. Another job I had was with Microsoft. I was in the sales team yet again.

Finally, in 2019, I graduated from RMIT University. After that, I received three to four job offers from different engineering firms. I chose one and stayed there for two months before deciding that it wasn't for me. I just didn't like it. I felt no passion for it. It didn't give me that feeling of being challenged and wanting to grow.

iv) That is a wide range of jobs! Now that you are in the business area, what do you consider as the top business / entrepreneurial skills?

Honestly, getting into business is 80% about your mindset. Of course, you need some skills. But it's mostly about having discipline. There'll be days when you won't feel like working, but you still have to. You need to show up every day and have the right attitude. That requires discipline and having the right mindset.

But in terms of the skills needed to build a successful business, the number one skill you need to have know is your money. I'm talking about cash flow and other financial metrics. The second one would have to be having a good, if not thorough, knowledge about sales. Without sales, there's no revenue. Without revenue, you can't do any project with your business.

Further to that point, I would say that being in sales is not only about being able to sell a product or service. It's also about selling yourself, selling who you are in terms of your beliefs and values.

Learning these skills comes with time. But reading a book is a great way to bridge the gap. I know some would say, *'Knowledge is power.'* But to that I say, *'Applied knowledge is power.'* The application of knowledge is the key to success.

Finally, in business, you really don't have to do it all alone. If you think that you're *'the man'* and you can do it all, trust me, you will not get anywhere. You need a team. You can be specialised in a specific area like sales just like I am, but you also need to know about the other aspects of running a business. These include business development and marketing. That will take you another four to five years of learning. Rather than studying again, you can try partnering with someone who has the skills you need. That's what I did in my business and it's worked for us. My team and I are committed to the same vision and we make it happen.

This was also the case back in university. I always partnered with committed students who strove to be at the top of the class. We challenged each other. And that's how I was able to get all my HDs in my degree.

v) What are your biggest learnings from the change that COVID-19 brought to our lives in 2020?

For me, the biggest learning is that life is going to test you constantly. Whenever that happens, you can choose to either stay where you are—which is practically downhill—or you can cope and grow. So, COVID has been a great challenge just like any other major event such as losing a loved one. You just need to have the right attitude and the discipline to persevere through these things.

As an engineer, I believe that every problem has a solution. I thought of COVID as a problem that presents an opportunity. So, just like any problem, you need to find a solution for it. And remember to have the discipline and attitude to persevere and stay positive. Work around things. Be flexible and adaptable. If you're not, you will simply lose.

vi) Do you have any parting thoughts for the 2021 graduates and beyond?

Well, I think it's a given that you should research a company you want to work for. Everyone knows why you should do it. But for me, I would emphasise on finding out who will be interviewing you. What are they like? What are their values? Then going back to the company, know what their work culture is. That's very important. As for yourself, determine what values and skills you bring to the table.

To end this, I'd like to say that work is probably 90% about attitude, especially your willingness to learn. So, remember to always stay positive and hungry.

vii) Thanks for your time and insights, Jamal. It's much appreciated. Finally, what is the best way to contact you?

You can reach me on Instagram, Facebook or LinkedIn under the same name: **Jamal Elamsy.**

4.1.4. Mahmoud Naser
RPA Lead, Deloitte Consulting

i) Thank you for taking the time to join us today. Tell us about yourself in terms of your background, namely educational and professional backgrounds.

My name is Mahmoud Naser. I currently work in the Intelligent Automation space with a focus on Robotic Process Automation (RPA).

As for my educational and professional journey, I started in telecommunication engineering in Jordan before I transferred my degree to Swinburne University in Melbourne. After finishing my studies, I got a graduate job with IBM in an automation team. Then a year later, I started my Master in Information Security and Assurance from RMIT. While at uni, I did a few different jobs like tutoring and IT support for the Australian Open and network admin with the great Bakers Delight.

My journey at IBM came to an end when I got the chance to do an exchange semester in Germany for my Master's degree. Upon coming back, I worked with Victoria Police on a research project for some time. I also tried my luck at a start-up for a year. Afterwards, I joined the ranks of consultants at Deloitte Consulting, where I have been for the past three years now.

ii) So, back to your university days, what was Mahmoud like as a grad? Did you always know what you wanted to do? What would you advise graduates in terms of career planning?

Regarding career planning, I had the idea that I wanted to work in telecommunications when I started my degree. I liked it. It was where I wanted to kind of build my degree. Other than continuing my studies, I had no concrete plans back then on how to achieve my goal. So, I just kept on studying.

As I started to work through my subjects at university, my learnings took me in a few different directions. Mainly, I found myself veering towards programming subjects. My interest in programming grew from there, so I shifted my focus from telecommunications to it. And that's what got me into my graduate job.

So when it comes to career planning, my message is that it's nice to have an idea of what you want to do. It would also be helpful to have a concrete plan on how you want to achieve it. But remember that your ideas and plans will be tested as you go through university, as you begin to realise and shape what you like and don't like through the subjects you take. Then other than your subjects, my advice is to talk to your professors and career counsellors as well. Attend career fairs, too. All of these will help you determine and shape your degree.

I'd also like to mention that I was lucky that Swinburne had a Work Integrated Learning (WIL) program. It's a program wherein they place you in a company for up to six months to a year. Such experiences do help you formulate where you want to go.

iii) Knowing what you know now, what did you do that worked and would you have done differently or expect graduates to have done?

I think one thing that I definitely caught on a bit later in my career is networking. So, I would've liked to attend more events to build my network, especially during events where people from my industry were present.

As you get into the industry, you start to realise the importance of networking. So, it would help if you started making contact with industry professionals even while you're still studying. You can meet them at job fairs and during career planning sessions. Send them a simple LinkedIn note after an event. It goes a long way.

My other piece of advice is to start a side project. Working on passion project sets you apart when you're competing with other graduates. This could be your project, one for a community you're volunteering in or an on-campus initiative you're passionate about. Such activities will show your future employer that you're a motivated person.

iv) In your career you have worked with start-ups, government departments and large enterprises. How do you compare such experiences and what would you advise graduates to do?

That's an interesting question. To answer that, I'm going to use one of my favourite consulting lines: it depends. It depends on what you want in terms of your career.

Government jobs do come with a certain level of safety. But that safety comes at the cost of your learning and career progression. Large enterprises may not provide the same level of security, but make up for it with a faster learning curve. Consulting and start-ups would probably give you the most rapid learning curve. They'll also give you the most exposure. However, these could come with a higher risk.

My advice for young graduates would be to focus on growth and exposure, as you would still have more energy and less responsibility. The risk factor wouldn't be as high as it'd be if you delayed working on these. So, a start-up or consulting are good choices.

This is the advice I got when I reached out to one of my favourite lecturers in Swinburne, Dragi Klimovski. He also noted that when changing jobs it's more comfortable moving to government and large enterprises than it is to move into start-ups and consulting.

So, those are things that you need to keep in mind once you graduate, prioritise on continuous learning and growth.

v) On that learning theme, as you did your Master's degree (post-graduate) part-time while working, should graduates do their Master's degree straight after finishing their Bachelor's, or start working first?

Just like in most fields, learning and upskilling are required within the technical areas. There are always companies looking for emerging technologies, so investing in those skills would significantly increase your employability.

Online course providers such as Coursera and Udemy are great platforms for this. The same goes for different technical meet-ups. They tackle emerging technologies such as automation, data analytics and artificial intelligence.

As far as studying a Master's degree, it's the right choice if you want to deepen your knowledge about a particular topic. However, based on personal experience, I invested a fair bit of time on it but ended up not entirely using it in the workplace. So, to answer your question, a Master's degree is not always the answer.

But back then, as a graduate, the consistent advice I got from career professionals is not to do it right after the Bachelor's degree.

So for soon-to-graduate students or new graduates who want to start their Master's, take note of the following:

1. You need to be in the industry for a while to get a better understanding of current trends. You need experience and exposure to be confident and comfortable with the choice of your Master's.

2. Your starting salary is more likely to increase with experience as opposed to a degree if you are applying for graduate jobs.

Taking up a Master's degree isn't a convenient journey. If you do it full-time, it would usually take a year or so. And if you study part-time, it would take much longer. So, you need to be armed with the right knowledge and information before you take this step.

vi) You mentioned that you are an RPA lead with Deloitte. For many graduates, RPA is an interesting field. Can you tell us what you do on a daily basis?

Absolutely. As I mentioned earlier, it stands for Robotic Process Automation. The idea here is to automate processes, with a focus on high-volume, low-complexity processes.

For example, when you apply for a debit card in the bank, you fill in the same form as everyone else. Afterwards, it goes to a team that stores the information. Then, they do a background check. Based on that, a team creates a record on the system and informs you about the result or confirmation.

This process is linear and straightforward. It's repetitive in high volume. There are a lot of people doing it at the same time. This is one of the kinds of processes that RPA will give you a good return on investment.

Another good example of this from recent times is when the Victorian Government announced the 5 km radius lockdown for Melbourne and not regional Victoria, there was an influx of applications to VicRoads (Government Road Authority) for Melbourne residents wanting to change their address to regional Victoria. That would have been an ideal process to automate, as scaling up the virtual workers would be more efficient in responding to the demand on time.

There are three main pillars in RPA: assessment, build and support. The first pillar is about identifying which processes to design in automation. The second pillar is the actual designing, building and testing of the solution. The third pillar is about how to monitor and maintain your digital workers once you build the automation.

My work is mostly in the second pillar, where I lead a team that builds and tests automation solutions. I'm responsible for checking their progress and documentation. I ensure that all the information we need to build the process is available by removing any blockers we face and escalating any issues.

vii) There is a lot of talk about technology post-COVID and how some processes will be automated. How do you see the sector shaping up? What skills or certificates would you advise graduates to focus on there?

So, RPA has always been growing rapidly, especially in the past few years. For example, Gartner expects the growth in the RPA market to be at double-digit rates through 2024!

The focus over the next few years would be to partner RPA with other technologies such as machine learning, data analytics, process flow management and other ones that can fill in the gaps that RPA can't, such as reading handwriting, image recognition and language processing.

How to upskill within this space? If you search about RPA, you will find several tools and consultancies available, each with their strengths, weaknesses training and certification programs that you can enrol in. Any of these will help get you into the RPA space.

Some of them are focused on the technical side, which is developing the actual automation. While others are focused on setting up that platform, or on setting up the capability within the organisation. So, it depends on what you want to do. RPA is interesting as it does mix and match between the business and technical aspects. This means that you don't need to be focused on just the technical or business part to work in the industry. You can combine both, depending on how you want to balance them.

viii) What are your biggest learnings from the change that COVID-19 brought to our lives in 2020?

As unfortunate as the pandemic is, one of the good things I still picked up and loved during this time is having more control of your day and time. While in lockdown, I started to wake up at 5:00 am to take a walk. I enjoy doing this along with being able to organise my day rather than waking up rushing to get ready to my first meeting. I was also blessed enough to get some morning quality time with my family.

Career-wise, I think enterprises as a whole have started to realise that remote working works. I mean, there are challenges, but it's something that we can use so anyone can work from anywhere. And this realisation seems to be catching on.

ix) Do you have any parting thoughts for the 2021 graduates and beyond?

Network, Network, Network. 100%! I think if I were a grad today, I would attend a lot more meet-ups within my industry. I will utilise LinkedIn a lot more as it's such a powerful tool, especially now when there are more people online than there was ever before. You have a broader and more responsive audience.

Another thing would be branding. If you have a side project, make sure you have a website for it. Mention your volunteer experience. Ensure that people get the impression that you intend to give out when they visit your profile.

x) Thanks for your time and insights, Mahmoud. It's much appreciated. Finally, what is the best way to contact you?

That would be through my LinkedIn account: **Mahmoud Naser**.

4.1.5. Param Artputhanathan

International Student Engagement Manager,
Monash University

i) Thank you for taking the time to join us today. Tell us about yourself in terms of your background, namely educational and professional backgrounds.

I grew up in Singapore and after completing my military service, I went to Malaysia to commence my studies in the Monash University Foundation Year. Upon completion of that program I arrived in Melbourne for my undergraduate studies.

I wasn't sure what to study at first. I enrolled in a business degree with a major in Banking and Finance. I also did an arts degree with a major in Politics.

For me, one degree was about passion and the other one was about the professional opportunities. That's always been my mindset as I come from a country where there isn't much government support. This means that even if you don't have a job, you're still on your own. It's your responsibility to make the right decisions.

I also recently completed my Master in International Relations (Trade and Diplomacy) given my interest in politics and international relations. During my undergraduate days, I was quite involved with the student association on campus. I believe the experience I gained from my student representation roles set the foundations for my current career.

It started when I saw a poster a week after orientation seeking a first year international student. Since I didn't know anyone in the country, I started getting involved with the aim to meet more people. I really loved the energy of our group. Everyone just wanted to have fun and create a good experience for others. By getting involved, I got to deal with many aspects of the organisation. Those included student administration, events and wider engagement strategies. My group and I stayed together for about four or five years. And now, I've got a great international network because they all went overseas.

Things weren't easy as I graduated just after the global financial crisis (GFC). So, it wasn't a surprise that I couldn't get a job in the field, especially since I didn't have citizenship or permanent residency.

Given the situation, I thought to myself, *'Why don't I look at what skills I have developed over the years and apply for jobs based on that?'* And that's what I did. I found myself in an interview with a higher education provider called Study Group. They wanted someone to look after the accommodation aspects of their college students. Based on my previous experience on campus, I was a good fit.

ii) So, what would you tell graduates who feel like they should have it all 'figured out'?

Well, to be honest, what I told you was just a summary of my journey. I know it may have sounded like everything flowed quite nicely, but that wasn't the case. I was actually worried during the last six months before my graduation.

I could see the economy going down. I could see fewer jobs advertised. My seniors also said that they were having trouble finding jobs. I wanted to apply to a bank, but banks were retrenching people, with one company reducing their staff by 3000!

It was scary. It was hard to pretend that I was confident. I was certainly in a doubtful space. But I also thought that the most important thing was not to stay in that space. I asked myself, *'What are you going to do about it? How are you going to overcome it?'* No matter how bad a situation is, you have to think about the solution. You have to think about how you can find your place in the midst of the current state of affairs.

Some people are more resilient than others. Resilience isn't something you learn as part of your degree. It's something you need to work on yourself.

iii) Knowing what you know now, what would you tell Param as a grad, and any future graduates, for that matter?

I would say, 'Be confident!' When you graduate, it can seem like it's all doom and gloom sometimes with economies going up and down. But even if you can't see what the future holds, you have to remember that things are going to improve. It definitely won't stay the same. Yes, it might go down again in another 5 or 10 years. But that's just part of how it works. So, make sure that you always have a plan of attack.

As for me, I didn't have a long-term plan. I had a short-term one, and this is what I'm going to do this year. But I think it's quite important to plan your career as well. Plans change and that's fine. But in planning, you will often find that you recognise certain skills and trends in the market that would be of interest to you.

Personally, I kind of like the way my career turned out. But to be clear, it's not because things were already set. Some things just happened as I was looking around for opportunities.

Given that, one thing that I always tell graduates is that depending on what you study and the industry you're in, things can diverge. So, if you're in one industry for too long, then that's all the experience you're going to have. If you want to change careers or industries, I suggest creating a plan to facilitate such a change.

iv) Given your student engagement background, what would you expect if you interview a graduate for your team?

I look out for skills that aren't part of one's degree. Things like soft skills are what I'm interested in. Of course, some basic technical skills like computer literacy are expected. Since we're relying more on technology, we're looking for people with skills like producing web content such as videos.

I also look at a person's level of communication skills. Can you hold a conversation? Do you only know how to communicate in text messages? Can you write a proper email or report? Can you effectively speak to people who are senior or junior to you?

During an interview, I think it's also important to try to bring out your personality. After all, it's still a human interaction so be yourself. This gives me an idea about how the person is going to fit within the team.

Also, before any job interview, do your research. Read up on the challenges the company may be facing. And think of ways on how you can contribute towards addressing those challenges. It also helps to learn about your interviewer. I've had people checking out my LinkedIn profile before coming in. While I'm not saying whether that's good or bad, and certainly doesn't influence the interview, it definitely shows that you're serious about the job. It tells me that you've done your research. You can also tap into your existing network and speak to others whom you may know in the industry. They might be able to offer you some insights that could assist you in your interview.

v) As an active international student on campus, what would you advise other international students who feel like they are at a disadvantage when applying for jobs?

First, in terms of being active on campus, I think it's essential to enable your success. For undergraduate students, this is so important. Know what services your university has. Those may include career services, student clubs and societies. Being active or getting involved isn't only about having fun, but also about establishing a network. We're so lucky because people from all parts of the world come to Australia to study, as I did. This allows you to create a great global network.

Regarding international students applying for a job in Australia, I don't believe they're always at a disadvantage. While there's a disadvantage when it comes to the visa, you can manage that by getting good advice from a registered agent. Other than that, you bring a unique set of skills that other people don't have.

You came from another country. You have a thorough knowledge of another culture. In most cases, you can also speak another language. Most importantly, you overcame a lot of personal challenges in adjusting to a new country. Present yourself with confidence by recognising your strengths. Use those as your selling points in your job search.

vi) What are your biggest learnings from the change that COVID-19 brought to our lives in 2020?

Well, it's been an interesting learning experience. This year has provided me with a lot of opportunities. I've learned many things and met so many people who had come together to address the needs that the crisis created.

When it comes to learnings, the most important things I've learnt is the need to constantly keep yourself motivated and the power of positive thinking.

You shouldn't be afraid of change. More importantly, take a break when you need it to recharge yourself.

Another important thing would be to have a routine. This is a piece of general advice that applies even before this pandemic. Having said that, I know that for those who already have a routine as I do, COVID-19 has either stopped or changed it. To address that, I've developed a routine at home, which has worked well for me, as it helps me to get in the right mindset for work.

vii) Thanks for your time and insights, Param. It's much appreciated. Finally, what's the best way to contact you?

That would be via my LinkedIn account: **Param Artputhanathan.**

4.2 Embrace The Journey!

Yes, I'm asking you (again) to embrace the uniqueness of your own graduate journey, and its relevant career prospects. In preparation for this book, I became curious to know how a career is defined, linguistically speaking. What did I do? I Googled it! The top result was from the Oxford Dictionary, and offered the following definition of career:

Career (noun): *an occupation undertaken for a significant period of a person's life and with opportunities for progress.*

Career (verb): *move swiftly and in an uncontrolled way.*

As you can see, even the dictionary can have different career definitions. What a good career means to you, may be different to what it means to another graduate or professional. Do not let someone else's journey dictate what you should do and how you should feel.

Embrace The Journey!

If you are reading this after graduation, it is possible that you finished your degree without going through the activities mentioned in Chapters 1 and 2. That is ok. Thousands of graduates do not go through them and eventually thrive in their careers. Your mission as a graduate is to increase your employability chances now, not to question what you could have done differently in the past.

Embrace The Journey!

I want you to know that whatever happens in the next few days, weeks, or even months, does not determine who you are, and it is not necessarily a reflection of your capabilities. Trust me when I say I've been there. The lack of clarity is daunting. Before I secured a job, for months I was frustrated with the process, thought that I had it all wrong and that I should study something else. I felt unemployable and lost. I assure you that such a feeling is normal and everyone eventually finds their way.

Embrace The Journey!

Whether you are GRAD 1, GRAD 2, or GRAD 3, let me tell you that the stress and frustration you might be having with your current job search will be nothing more than a distant memory in a few years. What you believe is a matter of life and death right now will be the least of your worries not long from today. Keep your head high and don't lose sight of the big picture.

Embrace The Journey!

The 2020 Graduate Outcomes Survey states that around 3 in 4 graduates find full-time employment within four months of graduation! So, you are a lot more likely to be employed than not. Be patient and persistent and you will be fine!

Embrace The Journey!

What you may end up doing for a job does not matter as much as you think. As a matter of a fact, a recent Gallup Study found that 85% of workers globally are disengaged in their workplace! I am not saying this to discourage you, but I am just suggesting you keep your perspective in check. Your first job might not be your best and almost certainly will not be your last.

Embrace The Journey!

Speaking of perspective, it is no surprise that the 9-5 job lifestyle varies greatly from your student life in terms of activities, time, and priorities. While you may be dying to get a job now, thousands if not millions of employees on the other end are counting the days to the next holiday. See the discrepancy? Your perspective is your superpower, so keep it in check.

Embrace The Journey!

Whether you have graduated with high grades or not-so-high grades, from a technical degree or otherwise, there is a place for you in the market. Do you think it's an exaggeration? Apple, Google, IBM, Netflix, and Tesla are examples of companies who removed the degree requirement completely from their recruitment, with many companies expected to follow. Present your skills and get the job!

Embrace The Journey!

The whole scope of this book has been about employability and jobs, but what about your own business? How is that for a job? There are thousands of resources out there, so seek knowledge from successful business owners, and make your dreams a reality. Whether your first 'business owner' job suits you or not, you will inevitably acquire more transferable skills in the process by the end of it, that you can deploy in your next business or job!

Embrace The Journey!

COVID-19 came as an unwelcomed surprise, not only to graduates, but also to experienced professionals. As this book goes to print in late 2020, the world interest rates are at an all-time low and the unemployment rate in many countries is on the rise. I am not saying this for you to think it's difficult to get a job. But it is important to understand what jobs are in demand in the post-COVID job market, so you can upskill accordingly.

Just like thousands of other graduates who eventually found jobs in similar circumstances (such as the 2008 GFC), you will get through this. You know that when you get a job in this challenging market, you can get a job in any market!

So, open your GradGate and soldier on. You are more employable than you think!

Taken at my graduation ceremony!

AFTERWORD

While I have long thought that my graduate journey is unique in many aspects, I came to realise that such struggles are not uncommon for most graduates. This was evident as I started to get more involved with graduates via **GradShip** through various consultations and workshops.

Although this book only came to light in late 2020, it has been a long time coming. As both of my younger siblings (Amal and Younis) were completing their degrees when COVID-19 was added to the mix, witnessing their struggles firsthand reinforced my desire to help.

Victoria's 2nd lockdown in 2020 meant that my last excuse of "not having time" could no longer be used, so The GradGate came to light shortly after that.

You have made it this far, and I genuinely appreciate the time you have invested in reading The GradGate. If you got some value out of this book, changed your perspective, or have feedback to improve the next edition, join **"The #GradGate Readers"** Facebook group where we discuss such topics, or contact me directly via LinkedIn or at:
yousef@gradship.com.au.

And yes, I would expect you to include an emoji or two! ☺

REFERENCES

1. Australian Government. "OS-HELP and overseas study." *Study Assist*, 2020, https://www.studyassist.gov.au/help-loans/os-help-and-overseas-study. Accessed 02 12 2020.

2. Australian Government. "Facts about studying in Australia." *Study Australia*, 2020, https://www.studyinaustralia.gov.au/English/Why-Australia/facts-about-studying-in-australia. Accessed 02 12 2020.

3. Australian Government. "Small Business Counts." *Small business in the Australian economy*, 2019, https://www.asbfeo.gov.au/sites/default/files/documents/ASBFEO-small-business-counts2019.pdf. Accessed 02 12 2020.

4. Bainbridge, Carol. "The Difference Between Being Shy and Being Introverted." *The Difference Between Being Shy and Being Introverted*, 18 07 2020, https://www.verywellfamily.com/the-difference-between-being-shy-and-being-introverted-1448616. Accessed 02 12 2020.

5. Belli, Gina. "CME Group." *At least 70% of jobs are not even listed*, 11 April 2017, https://www.businessinsider.com/at-least-70-of-jobs-are-not-even-listed-heres-how-to-up-your-chances-of-getting-a-great-new-gig-2017-4. Accessed 02 12 2020.

6. Berg, Madeline. "The Highest-Paid Actors 2019: Dwayne Johnson, Bradley Cooper And Chris Hemsworth." *Forbes*, 21 08 2019, https://www.forbes.com/sites/maddieberg/2019/08/21/the-highest-paid-actors-2019-dwayne-johnson-bradley-cooper-and-chris-hemsworth. Accessed 02 12 2020.

7. Black, Rosemary. "PSYCOM." *Glossophobia (Fear of Public Speaking): Are You Glossophobic?*, PSYCOM, 12 Sep 2019, https://www.psycom.net/glossophobia-fear-of-public-speaking. Accessed 02 12 2020.

8. Cambridge Dictionary. "Cambridge Dictionary." *Cambridge Dictionary,* 2020, https://dictionary.cambridge.org/dictionary. Accessed 02 12 2020.

9. DMR. "Business Statistics." *220 LinkedIn Statistics and Facts (2020)*, 2020, https://expandedramblings.com/index.php/by-the-numbers-a-few-important-linkedin-stats. Accessed 02 12 2020.

10. Edison Research. "The Social Habit 2019." *The Social Habit 2019*, 2019, http://www.edisonresearch.com/wp-content/uploads/2019/05/The-Social-Habit-2019-from-Edison-Research.pdf. Accessed 02 12 2020.

11. Glassdoor. "15 More Companies That No Longer Require a Degree—Apply Now." *Glassdoor*, 20 01 2020. https://www.glassdoor.com/blog/no-degree-required. Accessed 02 12 2020.

12. Jensen, Erin. "Dwayne Johnson, Taylor Swift, Gayle King, more cover Time's 100 most influential people issue." *USA Today*, 2019, https://www.usatoday.com/story/life/people/2019/04/17/taylor-swift-dwayne-johnson-cover-times-most-influential-people-issue/3484216002. Accessed 02 12 2020.

13. Jobvite. "Jobvite." *Jobvite Recruiter Nation Report*, 2016, https://www.jobvite.com/wp-content/uploads/2016/09/RecruiterNation2016.pdf. Accessed 02 12 2020.

14. LinkedIn. "The 2020 LinkedIn Opportunity Index." *LinkedIn | Economic Graph*, 2020, https://economicgraph.linkedin.com/research/opportunity-index-2020. Accessed 02 12 2020.

15. LinkedIn. "LinkedIn Blog." *More Than Just a Resume: Share Your Volunteer Aspirations on Your LinkedIn Profile*, 2013, https://blog.linkedin.com/2013/09/04/more-than-just-a-resume-share-your-volunteer-aspirations-on-your-linkedin-profile. Accessed 02 12 2020.

16. LinkedIn. "LinkedIn Blog." *Tuesday Tip: Stand Out by Flexing Your Skills on Your LinkedIn Profile*, 2018, https://blog.linkedin.com/2018/january/9/tuesday-tip-stand-out-by-flexing-your-skills-on-your-linkedin-profile. Accessed 02 12 2020.

17. M, Pushkarraj Jun 13·7 min rePushkarraj. "LinkedIn Algorithm 2020: All you need to know." *LinkedIn Algorithm 2020: All you need to know*, 2020, https://pushkarrajmehta.medium.com/hacking-the-linkedin-algorithm-in-2020-1e562149bd82. Accessed 02 12 2020.

18. Oxford Learners Dictionaries. "Oxford Learners Dictionaries." *Oxford Learners*, 2020, https://www.oxfordlearnersdictionaries.com. Accessed 02 12 2020.

19. Porchlight. "State of the Global Workplace." *State of the Global Workplace*, 19 12 2017, https://www.porchlightbooks.com/product/state-of-the-global-workplace_2--gallup-gallup. Accessed 02 12 2020.

20. Quality Indicators for Learning and Teaching. "Graduate Employment." *Graduate Employment*, 2020, https://www.qilt.edu.au/qilt-surveys/graduate-employment. Accessed 02 12 2020.

21. Southern, Matt. *40% of LinkedIn Members Visit the Site Every Day, Engagement is up 60%*, 2019, https://www.searchenginejournal.com/40-of-linkedin-members-visit-the-site-every-day-engagement-is-up-60/292579. Accessed 02 12 2020.

22. Wikipedia. "List of presidents of the United States by previous experience." *List of presidents of the United States by previous experience*, 2020, https://en.wikipedia.org/wiki/List_of_presidents_of_the_United_States_by_previous_experience. Accessed 02 12 2020.

AUTHOR'S BIOGRAPHY

YOUSEF SHADID

Yousef is the Founder of GradShip, an organisation that specialises in enhancing graduates' employability in Australia. Since founding GradShip in early 2020, Yousef has utilised his personal and professional experience to deliver hundreds of consultations, webinars and workshops to graduates and students alike.

Earlier in his career, Yousef pursued a Business Management degree that led him to work for Deloitte and EY Australia. Throughout his degree, Yousef used his time to assist and engage with students in the capacity of O-Host leader and mentor. He was also Swinburne's Abroad Ambassador upon his return from studying abroad on two occasions.

Due to his on-campus and subsequent professional involvement, Yousef was named a Swinburne Emerging Leader, and featured in the Top 50 Australian Professionals Magazine.

Lightning Source UK Ltd.
Milton Keynes UK
UKHW010639170822
407432UK00002B/500